Notes of a Dominatrix

by K. Allen

published Flying Finish Press

ISBN 978-0-6151-6606-3

to my many loves

Contents

I found him on the Internet chattering away. We had like minds. My boldness was attractive and I seemed to promise fun. First as friends. Later as lovers. I listened. He had a choice between what he wanted and what I needed him for. He laid down onto my bed. I never considered refusing. Scotch, scented oil, black leather and him; lying there in the half-light. He's so very male.

Move slowly. Wait until he has accepted this before you move on. No pretenses; there's nothing you can hide now. He knows me. It takes some courage to run without the social mask. To come out from behind that nice suburban image. To be known for who you are. By almost everyone. They all leapt too far. They think I deal in pain.

It must amuse him. How I signal willingness without a word and yet he knows he has to invite me before anything occurs. He commands the start and the stop. Power shifts. Yet we remain separate persons for all that we are together. Thus far. No further. We are all of us too fragile for more. Dreams must end. Lives lying in ruins.

We endure. Playing together, separately and in company. We are social in another sphere. My interlocking lives. Rapaciousness scheduled. Rampant lust time regulated. Few questions. Few answers. Always deep satisfaction just in his company. Contentment resting in his fur.

Flying down the cathedrals of the night
At one with all
At one with you

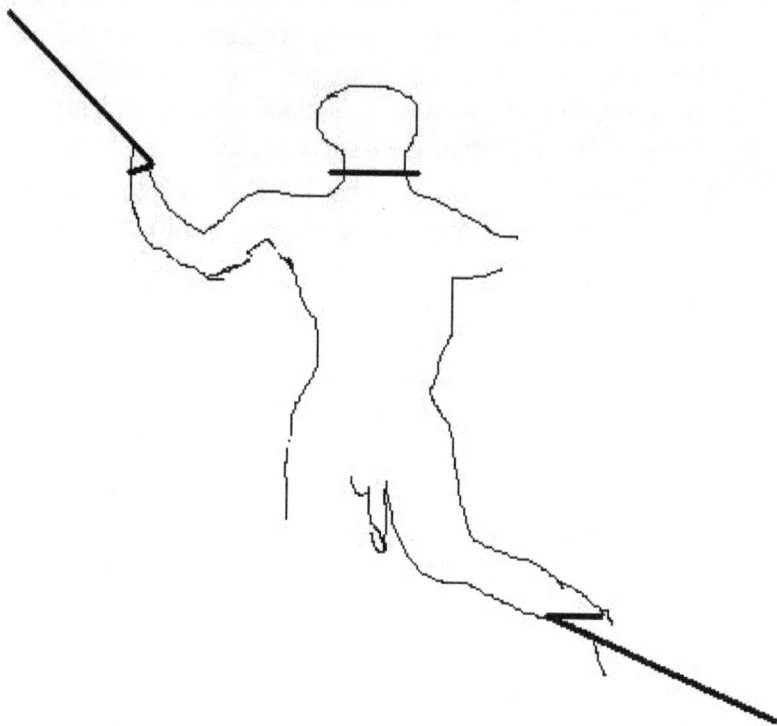

45 minutes only, continuous stimulation, how many full orgasms? Interesting concept—the multi-orgasmic male. There's the question of sensitivity and hydration. Option to refuse, of course. Might prove too intense.

4 orgasms obtained, sensitivity was an issue, incoherent

Seems jumpy

Very tactile, enjoys caressing—giving and receiving, tends to be a trifle fast.

Now this one is interesting. Dom to all but me. Fascination? Very oral, very vocal—flings off his clothes— exuberant? Has a great attitude. Commits errors—will not last. Settled for what he has.

Amazing lover! Galahad Complex. Very nice man, lovely to look at too. Friends now.

Begin by tying one wrist, and when comfortable with that, then tie up the opposite ankle. Slowly go on as comfort and trust develops. If you RUSH it, you've LOST it.

They all expect whips and chains, harsh words, mistreatment at my hands. So not me. Strap-ons are okay but I want to see his face so will use the legs up position next time. Then I could also play with his penis and testicles while having him. I think my vibe would work better.

The vibe works very well, orgasm reported to be intense. Lube and start it before entering. Continue to hold onto it.

Buy more scotch.

Cigars?

Evil seduction

I wish he'd tell me

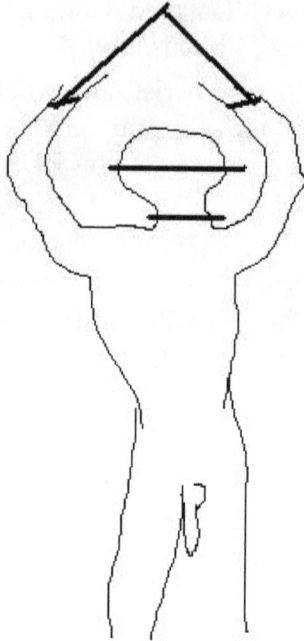

Blindfolded, hands cuffed and tied, only hands, two women, leather glove on one hand each, claws on the other hand, absolute silence. Caress everywhere but his penis, agonizingly slowly, until he begs.

He begged. He was so wound up he came when I lightly cupped his testicles so I milked him onto his belly, then she and I took turns sitting on his face. We let him up after 45 minutes. He was exhausted but very, very pleased. Loved it!

I collared him today. Lovely black and silver v-neck collar, just for him. My first male slut/sex slave. Then we went for lunch, fresh raw oysters. Delicious. Opened right before your eyes served on shell with lemon and some kind of red sauce—hot sauce? Maybe. The tag on his collar reads Slut 1.

My next slut/sex slave—prospective coming along well—needs more careful handling.

10

MFM with my two males. Slut 1 asked Slut 2 why he, 2, was still wearing the training collar. "What's up with that?" Magnificent afternoon! Driving back, Slut 2 asked about his collar. Knew that was coming. Crossed signals that evening. Partner used not into it so had to switch modes. Bad business – might ruin him.

Collared Slut 2. Looks very nice. Very arousing sight.

You have to get the proportions right else they do not look good. Slut 2 needed a wider, slightly, collar. See selection at PetSmart – Rottweiler section.

My demands are few. Keep me well contented sexually, keep me informed and wear condoms when with others. Their subjugation is private between us. They will not wear their collars in public. I expect them to be men, not leash puppies.

They look so appealing in their bathrobes smoking cigars after sex. Excellent idea

Love their fur too

I think I will keep them.

Begin as you mean to go on so decide up front what role you intend for him to play in your life: husband, FWB, friend w/o B, fuckbuddy, primary, secondary, tertiary, or whatever. Work that relationship out with him—nicely; you cannot beat him into it remember. (Yes I know how tough that can be.) Where did he ever get the idea that 'femininity' equaled (in all cases) meekness, timidity, and being weak, frail, or reluctant to have sex?

In any true D/s relationship, it is the submissive who has the power. At a word, the submissive stops the play. Responsible Doms and Dommes know this. Part of the enjoyment of such relationships is the shifting of power between the parties involved.

"In the end, it's up to you to weigh the pros and cons of such a relationship and decide if it is right for you right now. Let's see, the promise of mind-blowing sex with an experienced, confident woman, without the expectation of a long-term commitment... I know, it's a tough call. Be advised, however, that she's not going to put up with any masculine BS from you. Remember who you're dealing with and who your competition is. You're playing in the 'majors' now, guy, so you had better be prepared to leave the little league kid stuff behind you.

Slut 2 is being a bit 'high maintenance'. Dramatic.

I usually just wander over after maintaining eye contact, stand very close, put my fingertips under his chin near his mouth, and whisper "Hello." just before I kiss him. Seems to work.

Last night the silken slow sliding down your body finding that which made you quiver and catch your breath in delight slow very slowly twining around your shoulders your waist your loins feeling you against my cheek your skin and fur on my skin until I too quiver and burn with a predatory desire kissing caressing licking hearing your pleasure the black leather cuffs on your wrists the strap around the bedpost restraining your arms kissing up and along nuzzling enjoying you purrrrrrrrrr bless and be blessed.

From AskMen; bad advice!

Keep the power

"Ever been on a date and you could just sense that she had all the POWER? As if she had something that you desperately wanted and she KNEW IT? Most guys give away their power when they're with a woman. But do you think women are ATTRACTED to men who do this? No. The solution is to let her know that YOU are the one doing the "selecting," NOT HER. Show that you're picky about who you spend your time with and tease her about how she's screwing up her chances with you. Communicate that she's going to have to be on her best behavior to "qualify" for your time, and you'll be surprised just how far she'll go to get on your calendar."

Put yourself on a pedestal

"How would you act if you KNEW beyond the shadow of a doubt that a woman was TOTALLY into you but you weren't THAT interested in her, and that you decided RELUCTANTLY to give her a chance to hang out with you? What if you were a bit arrogant, but still in the mood to have fun with it and tease her to see how much she really wanted you? Practice coming from this mental space and you'll find that it'll eliminate your nervousness—INSTANTLY—and it will give you the edge you need to project a confident, attractive vibe to ANY woman."

Be TOO comfortable

"When a man is intimidated by a woman, she ALWAYS knows. How? Because he'll behave in ways that subtly tell her he's not comfortable with himself, with her and with the situation. The solution is to go to the OPPOSITE EXTREME and create the feeling that you're TOO comfortable. Mimic something she's doing in a funny way—for example, if she has a really rigid posture, sit up extra straight and say, "I really think you should work on

your posture." People are only playful like this when they're feeling comfortable, so this behavior will send the message that you're not intimidated by her in the slightest.

You can also pick up something small like a napkin and swat her with it, especially after you've made fun of her and she's pretending the comment bothered her. Most men don't have the guts to be this bold, so when you DO, she'll see you as a cut above other guys."

Bring out her animal responses.

"In the animal kingdom, different animals have signals that tell their mate of choice they're interested. When the male uses one of these signals, the female actually becomes PARALYZED and freezes in a sexually aroused position. Women respond in a similar way to several specific behaviors from men. So if you want to turn her on in a BIG way, smell her neck and shoulders... pull her hair gently by running your hand up the back of her neck and her hair, then make a fist and pull lightly... breath in her ear and whisper a compliment to her or bite her neck gently. Warning: Use these moves with caution—you may create a WILD animal that will stop at nothing to get what she wants from you."

Try any of these with me, guys, and you will be alone within 5 seconds. Remember, any such disrespect and I will have NO problem forgetting your name.

Most men would benefit from association with a soft domme. She has to know how to subtly wield power, how to signal the right cues, how to select potential partners—for unlike her whip-swinging sisters, she cannot coerce obedience. Only by beguiling—using their own desires to subjugate them—can she demand obedience. The giving and withholding of pleasure. How does one earn trust and respect if one cannot coerce it? Doesn't there always have be the idea of punishment for non-compliance? Yes, but for her, the soft dome, the punishments are limited to three:

1. Withholding pleasure
2. Ignoring him for a time
3. Forgetting him forever, leaving him his collar as a reminder of loss

Soft = no pain, no abuse & no humiliation

Hard = pain, abuse & humiliation including public humiliation

If I cannot 'take it', I will not 'dish it out'.

Look, guys; can we talk?

You all have not been getting the message:

1. I don't play games. I may periodically give way to excessive cuteness but it fools no one is not meant to fool anyone.

2. I do not give nor do I receive pain, abuse, or humiliation. So save the 'slap-happy, spanky, spanky games' for your others.

3. I am not a Goddess. I am a Demoness. There is a difference.

My feline persona has been developed over the last few years and is based upon direct observation of various actual *felis domestica*. Their natural love of sex combined with an inherent dignity and arrogance is consistent with my own personality so it was a natural fit. But there was a problem. While I want to be totally bewitching and beguiling and rock a man's senses into a whirlwind of delight—I am doomed to just being 'cute'. Even worse, I have been informed that I am 'adorable'. ARRRGH! Very disappointing for a girl! Why won't you men cooperate??

Up to three Sluts now.

All very nice men.

More bad advice:

Make her jealous

"If you really want to make sure you don't end up in the permanent friend zone after becoming her confidant, you must make her jealous of the other women in your life. Don't be entirely at her beck and call—keep dating other women. Let her know this, especially if the women you are dating are the sort she doesn't get along with. She will wonder why you'd rather be with them than with her". **PFFFT my advice is to ignore all such efforts. Say "how nice for you" and remain totally unimpressed.**

"I certainly understand the inclination to feel protective of your woman. Being a guy yourself, you are all too familiar with man's predatory nature. So how do you distinguish between the dogs who are really out for your girl and those whose ill intentions are the product of your distorted imagination?" **What's this "your woman" crap? And who says that only guys are 'predatory' *EG*? He only has the rights she grants him—nothing more.**

"Women look at a man's education level, his physical height and his salary level to determine if he's doing well enough in each category. This is how women choose the best mate." **She will if children are involved but if procreation is not the issue, OTHER variables are much more important.**

Every now and again, men give other men, good advice. But I am firmly convinced that most men have no idea about women mainly because they do not listen to women or to women's bodies. With a dominatrix, a man must listen so he learns very quickly the fine art of paying attention to her and of reading her body language.

Alcohol has a tendency to limit blood flow. This can work both ways 1. to prevent getting erections and 2. to make erections longer lasting. I also believe that a 'stunned' male only feels about half of what you do to him which also makes his erections last longer, and your 'job' harder? A few drinks = okay but 6 drinks = no, no.

Just because the woman is 'dangerous' does not mean she is any less feminine than other women.

1. **Always be respectful**
2. **Comply without being obsequious**
3. **Remain responsible for your emotions and behaviors**
4. **Be an adult**
5. **Abandon fear**

Not many like sexually aggressive straight women. Yes, I know what you all SAY but when the rumps hit the sheets, frequently it is another story. I've had guys disappear on me in the interval between the bar and the hotel! Driving along and then POOF he's gone! WTF? Amazing. All of these men complaining about not getting enough. JEEZ!

Sometimes I wonder about men—they're so scatter-brained!

Mixes for scented body oils
Mine: attar of roses and tabac
His: cedar and geranium/carnation
Not for internal/private area use

Go for full sensory overload next time—he's ready for it

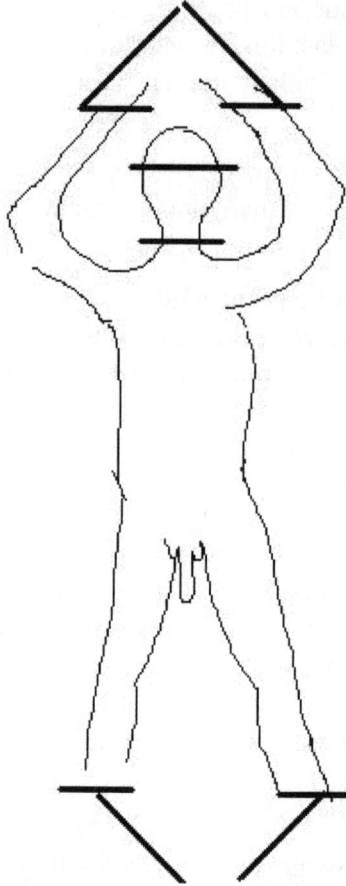

I love kissing him when he's tied like this. Know he cannot refuse nor escape—mmmmm very arousing!

He looks so good in the leathers too.

Very delicious!

No gags as I want his mouth available.

I'm all for equal time. Fair is fair. Only he is not interested in wielding power within a relationship so; his choice!

"Relationships, even the freedom-oriented ones, are based on give-and-take and a solid sense of equality. So if you're planning to date several men at once, don't get all bent out of shape when he dates several women; by playing

the field, you're giving him the license to do the same. In fact, it may be in your best interest to actually encourage such behavior... provided it's subtle. You're equals in everything, and if you're going to play around, so can he. It's simply a matter of keeping everything pointed in the right direction.[1]

Relationships do change over time so be prepared to accept change as the relationship develops.

Maintain your private space. No moving in; unless he swings too in which case you two can work it out on your own. Three bedrooms? One for you two only then his playroom and her playroom? Bowls of condoms tastefully displayed on the mantelpiece?

"The Grafenberg Spot is an area on the front wall (toward the tummy) of the vagina, between the opening and the cervix, generally 2 to 3 inches inward from the opening. Theory dictates that the G-spot can be one of two things: either a bundle of nerves coming from the clitoris, or a gland (or series of glands) that produces lubrication, or both. Now, while all women own a spot with a G, not all of them find G-spot stimulation pleasurable. Just as with the clitoris, some women are more than eager, while others do not like it whatsoever. It is very sensitive. Only time will tell. Insert a finger (or two) into the vagina with your palm facing her mons pubis gently; bend your fingers frontward so that they lightly stroke the front wall of the vagina. Varying the degree of pressure also helps."

"There are actually two types of multiple orgasms: sequential multiples and serial multiples. It can be difficult to tell the difference between the two—even for the woman. Distinguishing one type from the other is a matter of timing: Sequential multiple orgasms occur several minutes after one another, with an interruption in the

---

[1] *askmen.com*

arousal period in between, whereas serial multiples are separated only by seconds, producing one extended wave of pleasure. The latter is the truly rare form of the two."[2]

The sex improves upon further acquaintance as he learns you and you learn him and both of you RELAX around each other.

"As many professionals say, chemistry is the result of "positive vibrations" between two people. Obviously, there is some debate as to what exactly creates these vibrations, but most agree that attraction is amplified when we feel comfortable around someone. Negative vibrations arise from disagreements, overactive egos, competitiveness, and so on. Positive vibrations come about from being fun and exciting, conversing easily and effortlessly, and listening with an interest and a smile. Just sit across from her and act more comfortable than if you were at home in your plush recliner."

What I will ask, why I ask that, and what I am looking for when vetting men.

The process begins as soon as I see you and no you do not have to be Brad Pitt, et al. I'm looking at how you stand and how you move more than how you look. Fur is a definite plus.

Does he identify and approach me with confidence?

We all know why we are meeting and if he can't "get it up" here chances are he will not be able to "get it up" there.

The conversation is important for not only what he says/how he says it—but also for how much of the "heavy lifting" he leaves to me. Equal talk time is perfect.

1. How long have you been online dating/ how many met?

---

[2] *from Women. A Primer for men.*

Experience level questions. Also trying to gauge interest level. Standard sort of basic qualifying questions you'd get when applying for any position.

2. What do you particularly like, sexually?

Forget what you think I want to hear and just go for it. I will not be shocked, amazed, or injured by whatever you tell me. *EG* I promise. Besides, I may know someone who is looking for just that.

3. What do you do?

Nevermind any stereotypes. Just how much chaos can you take? Analytical or no? What you do for a living tells me how your mind generally works.

4. What are your interests/hobbies?

All work and no play—so just relax and tell me you're really into stamp collecting.

5. The standard marital status, kids, mode of living questions. Meaning how much time you have available and is daytime or evening good for you?

If you're married I might ask if she might like to play too but will not pry any further. That's your problem, buddy.

6. Do you have any questions?

If you do ASK! I understand this is your first time with us. Having questions is only to be expected.

Frankly, you men are REALLY spazzy!
Begin with:
"Why do women play hard to get?"
"its human nature to value people that you've invested resources on."
Then add in this gem,
"Why else would we endure hours of trivial female chatter and pick up the check at the end of it? There is no other reason than the hope that we will somehow convince her to go to bed with us."

toss in this item:

"If you're in an exciting relationship, don't let it last too long."

And you get a guy who will say this:

"You say: Honey, I'm going to watch the game over at Tim's place."

She says: *"What for?"*

Your reply: *"Because I enjoy watching the game with my buddies. See you later."*

and NOT expect to get this in reply:

She says: *"You won't see me later."*

(unless they're married where, as soon as he's left, she's on the phone jacking up his life insurance coverage – j/k)

SO ANGRY I WANTED TO:

put my fist through plate glass window somewhere

or

run over a puppy deliberately

or

spit

But do I actually do any of these? No. What I really did do was drive out, adhering to the speed limit, and fill up the trucks' gas tanks and then nicely drove back home again. Did this twice since there are two trucks and it was my turn. Sedate behavior masking rage.

Feeling 'dramatic' does not mean you have to act 'dramatic'.

Male Selection Tips:

For those who do not yet have a partner, here are some tips to use when you set out to find one.

Other than appealing to you to the point where you are wondering how his hands and lips would feel on your skin, you have to carefully consider several other criteria when selecting a male slut or when selecting a male to turn into a slut.

1. Can he get his mind around the concept of any woman, at any time he is required, anyway she wants him? Can he be passed around amongst the ladies like a six-pack? Would he enjoy it?

2. Does he have the *cajones* to submit without being obsequious or fawning? You want a man not a dog after all.

3. Is he presentable? If all you wanted was a penis, you could go buy one. Can he converse and how are his manners?

4. Is he willing to learn and open to new ideas and experiences?

5. Does he genuinely like women? You know what I mean by that—and yes, we can tell if he does.

Now all we have to consider is his amount of available free time, transport, and wherewithal (since you do not want to end up having to support him). Self-sufficient but willing men with the necessary free time are what you want. If he volunteers, that's even better!

Guy; you had a woman interested in you. What more did you really need to know?

All males should be checked for the following physical attributes during the vetting process.

- stands straight indicating a strong lower back
- walks with a free and easy stride
- fully articulating hips, knees, and shoulders
- flexibility especially through his waist
- manual dexterity
- enough rhythm to do a slow foxtrot (extra points if he can rumba)

The strength testing will come later.

"That's a little cruel, I think, but there's a grain of truth there....older women know that their physical beauty is fading fast, and that their chances of attracting a life partner diminish with every passing year. Add that to the common (but hardly universal!!!) attitude that they somehow "need" a man to "take care" of them (financially, emotionally...and yes, sexually), and you get the "clingy" response. If they find one they like, they tend to latch on because they're not at all sure they'll find another one.

This makes it sound like I think all older women are desperate, man hungry manipulators, and that's not at all the case. At my age, most of the women I meet might fit the definition of "older" and most of them are truly beautiful people. Sexually speaking, Ben Franklin was right, too....there is definitely something to be said for a woman who is flattered by the attention of a good man, no longer inhibited by the naiveté of youth, and determined to prove that there's life in an "aging body" – **which I find ironic as the man who wrote this is an older guy: proving there's still life in his aged body, perhaps??**

"mmmmm, possibly?...I'll take that as wild interest." LOL Very funny because Yes, guys do that! And it is CUTE!

"I know you want to be the master and in control of the situation at all times. But I believe your misunderstood as to what "you" really want. I also think no one's looked deep enough into you to know you."

Unfortunately guys do this as well! *smacking this guy upside the head* THINK BEFORE YOU WRITE, DAMMIT! Read my blog BEFORE e-mailing me. It will save you from getting so many heavy blows to your head. (Blunt objects optional.)

This view of his is based upon the belief that women do NOT know what they want as well as some guy they never even met and two that all controlling women are just RIDDLED with insecurities that can only be expressed in the 'right' situation, i.e., as a submissive to him.

NEITHER of those applies to me. After messing with men for more than 38 years—yeah, I do know what I like and my insecurities have been faced.

On Masculine Persistence:

Short answer is: No. Persistence usually ends up with them being blocked if not merely ignored and deleted without reading.

The long answer is: He can ask and ask and ask but hell will freeze over before I acknowledge his existence because he is most unsuitable and does not and never could meet my needs, desires, passions, or requirements because he's either too young, too stupid, too inept, too needy, too damn far away, too damn ugly, too controlling, or just too much of a huge pain in the ass to deal with (pauses for breath) or just too damn annoying for any woman to deal with, let alone a demanding woman like me, for any length of time which he will ever realize or understand because he's too stuck on himself and what he wants to consider the wishes of anyone else.

Enough said? *EG*

Gently, slowly, lightly
tracing graceful arabesques
with the tips of my nails and
fingertips over the contours
of your body as we lay side
by side naked upon your bed
in the half lit quietude after
passion. My lips lightly trail-

ing the movements of my hands, exploring you, tasting you enjoying the feel of your skin and fur, enjoying your scent. Will you come to me?

The hunger never goes away. I can feel it coming off of your skin as I walk over to where you're sitting on the barstool. Standing there between your knees I lift your chin with my fingers and lightly kiss you, lingeringly. You do not move. You do not speak. You accept the kiss, the subtle touch of our lips. Will you come to me?

"Arranging her skirts, she straddled my lap facing me on my sofa. She was so beautiful. Her eyes laughed and sparkled. Her lips curved delightfully and when she kissed me so lightly all of the desire I had for her flared up. Delicately kissing my lips over and over making me quiver. When she lifted her face away I became aware of the collar around my neck. I said nothing as she began undoing my shirt buttons and running her hands through my chest hair, caressing me. I stopped her hands at my belt buckle. It was too soon for me. Yes, I wanted her. But between wanting and having there lay issues. A messy past, an uncertain future, and a woman I barely knew snuggling into my arms as I wore her collar around my neck. There was that ring on her left hand. Where did that put me? Yes I wanted her, who wouldn't, but I am not a young guy heedless of consequences. No, not tonight. But you know I was kicking myself as I went upstairs to bed after watching her drive off.

What I wanted was not what she could give. What I wanted, she already had. Where did that leave me? Yes, she's a domme' but I haven't seen a whip yet. She seems kind and patient. I like her as a person and I care about her as a friend. But what am I getting myself into? She wants me? A beautiful woman wants me? And here I am somewhat bewildered since I am not a young tall hard-bodied hunk who's hung like a horse. I am not bad but she could have any man she really wanted. I am not rich either. She must just like me for some reason. What do I know about women? I tried to resist but then she was sitting next to me on my sofa. she had my shirt off and she ran her fingertips slowly and lightly up my spine and blew gently on the nape of my neck and lightly licked my ear.

Okay, okay, I give in! Take me upstairs to my bed! She did. I did. We did. Still no whips. She doesn't need them. Force of personality, drop dead sexy beauty, razor intelligence, and a skill at seduction that you have to experience to believe makes coercion unnecessary. Yeah, I am her slut. My former reluctance makes me smile."

Such a lovely teddybear of a man, I quite adore him!

No, it isn't anything about what he looks like etc., etc., etc.—it is the vibe that came off of him. Perhaps it is pheromones? It happens so very rarely but somehow the man just SPEAKS to me and I am powerless to resist! I MUST HAVE HIM NOW!!!

So, darling just lay down right here.

You're at some venue, having a good time, when so-and-so walks in. What do you do? You leave the party, bar, whatever—fleeing the scene! *"I just don't want to deal with it!"* You'd rather stop having fun just in case Mr. Annoying PITA decides he may want to throw a fit or make a dramatic scene than let him make a fool out of himself and, by inference, of you. TSK, TSK, TSK

My favorite way of dealing with these guys is to watch them, in silence, while they throw whatever tantrum they have chosen as if I was watching some very boring Congressional hearing on some very arcane bit of tax law. YAWN. You then ask if he really did enjoy publicly embarrass-ing himself like that. You then remind him that *"Hell buddy, I'm not married to you. Take it to someone who cares."* Then watch him turn red and disappear. Nothing to do with you. If he cannot behave like a gentleman then he doesn't deserve being treated like one. And he certainly shouldn't curtail your fun.

Meet at bars attached to restaurants. Then if you hit it off, you can ease on over for appetizers or dessert or maybe even an entire meal if you two hit it off without any distractions from the conversation. Walk her to her car, wrap her in those nice arms of yours firmly, give her a 'bad boy' grin, and a decent lingering kiss lasting at LEAST 20 seconds. Then let her take it from there.

MOST of the time.....but there are those times when a man had better just lie down and enjoy it because the lady's hungry and she's not going to accept any fuss or excuse. You don't want me to break a claw! The question is..............how much and how long of a fight are you going to put up?

Stump removal and the sheer bull-labor involved is what got me. Axe swinging is not my forte'. But to have those two large males standing there with huge grins on their faces while watching me and thinking, "she's so cute;" men can be very exasperating. Pat the cute fluffy bunny on her head and shoo her away.

It is a good thing I like these two.

Went shopping with Slut 2 in DuPont Circle—interesting BDSM for gay men shop—they damn near died when I—a real woman!—walked in. they had some very attractive outfits for Slut 2 on display but he was feeling timid so I just bought a pair of padded ankle cuffs.

How to Introduce Him to Your Kinky Side:
1. **Sit on his lap facing him; kiss him while deftly sliding a collar around his neck.**
2. **Leave a collar out on the coffee table.**
3. **Use your vibe as 'the second man.'**
4. **Run your hand up the back of his neck into his hair. Tilt his head back and kiss the base of his throat, gently but lingeringly.**
5. **When hanging out naked in the house wear stilettos.**

GRRRR

1. If you'd rather talk to Jim than have sex with me, you might as well put a bullet through your brain because you are done. "It's dead, Jim." But it was an important personal matter! Yeah, well, this is a party. You do know about parties, yes?

2. No condoms = no sex and I don't give a damn about your previous 35 years of just getting shots to fix you right on up, hun. How many times does it take getting run over before you learn NOT to play in the street?

3. Yes most women have a nice slow pace and want to be caressed and cajoled into having sex with men they want to know something about. That's MOST WOMEN, mind

you, not THIS WOMAN. Once my engines have been spun up and the blood's roaring—just lie down right here and shut up.

Yes, you all may comment and I may bite back but then – you know I love you all dearly – this week.

So other than throwing his ass over the balcony railing—what else was I do to?

Obviously this is an in-experienced male. Because any sensible male knows that a woman doesn't hit her sexual peak until in her 40's and that a self aware and sexually aggressive woman easily out-guns any six men you'd care to name. You ladies are just not educating your men properly!

Women ask men impossible to answer questions because the question we actually asked is not the question we really want answered. You only have to lie if you answer the question we actually asked rather than the one we really want answered. You would not have to lie if you ignored the question we actually asked and answered the question we really wanted answered. This is especially true if the question we actually asked requires the man to give an opinion in his answer which is never permitted. (If a man gives a woman his opinion on any topic he should immediately apologize and humbly beg her forgiveness unless said opinion deals directly with automobiles or power tools.) Be advised that women ask these questions as a test. We are determining your ability to read subtext, deciding whether to continue the relationship or not, and seeing how clever you really are as shown by the quality of your answer. You will remember that women are naturally more sibylline than men and that we enjoy playing that delightful game "Confuse-A-Male". This has been a test. This has only been a test. If this had been an actual emergency requiring an opinion we would have asked a woman.

"Women need to realize that their bodies are temples—or at least men like to think so—and that they shouldn't be shared with any Tom, Dick or Harry. Once a woman realizes this, three things will happen:

1. She'll appreciate herself a lot more, and in turn the man will gain more respect for her and realize that he has a valuable treasure.

2. The man who had to work hard and commit in order to bed a woman will appreciate her more. After all, time was invested in her.

3. The sex will be brought to a whole new passionate level when she finally makes love to the man who fought for her—by being patient.

Today too many people—including myself—place too much importance on sex. This explains why so many marriages don't work. People base their whole relationship on sex and don't realize that when the passion disappears, and the honeymoon phase dies down, there is nothing left but each other's flaws."

This article was in response to a woman asking why men have issues with a promiscuous woman. She said "I was honest, told him the truth when he asked how many men I had slept with, and then I never heard from him again." All of the above is nonsense. Promiscuous women are not those with low self-esteem. They are fun-loving women who view sex as joyous rather than debasing. We are all people here; just trying to get along as best we can. Treating each other kindly and with respect, unless they demand otherwise, will go a long way to improving all of our lives. Of course sex is important! No, you're just left with their flaws. Their virtues remain as well.

His sexual subjugation should be joyous and life affirming. This somewhat less than silken dalliance should be fun for both with each one pleasing the other. This result cannot be achieved without mutual regard and respect. There also has to be a mutual sexual attraction. If the blood is not roaring within, then nothing good can come of playing in this fashion. In many ways, the actual acts are the same and only the perspective changes. Fellatio becomes feeding off the male, for example, when done from a female superior position. The male takes on the passive role during sex unless called upon to please his lady. While there are no set rules, play should be mutually satisfying with both having orgasms. There are men who can wear a collar and leash with a great deal of panache. I have seen this. He was wearing only a 'bad boy' grin and sitting on my sofa at the time.

Hey there, care to roll around in the long grass? Big strong males who can withstand my passions like you shouldn't be afraid. I may even turn a delightful shade of pink and purrrrrrrrrrrrrrrrr.

I might want to tie you up and see where your hot buttons are. I love it when a man can neither resist nor escape and I can do whatever I want. Hmmmm. Kiss there, lick over here, caress this and that especially that. And if the kitten wants some cream.... well that's always 'on tap' as it were now isn't it?

Can you truly acquiesce to being used for my pleasure alone without regard for your own? Can you lie there, naked in the half light, passively awaiting your fate? Perhaps even trembling with desire beneath the caress of my claws and fangs as I meander all over your body with agonizing slowness? Will you beg for your orgasm? Shall we see how much 'stimulation' you can take?

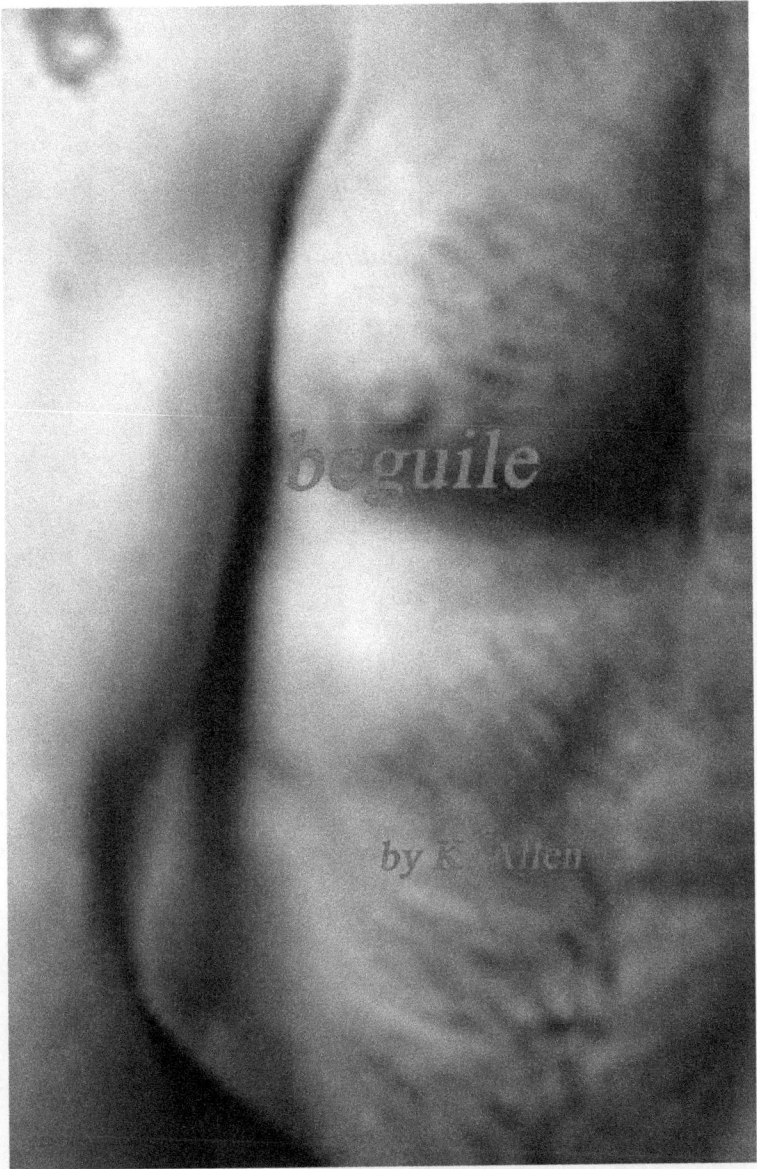

photograph by Corbis

35

beguile: to manipulate through the use of charm,
to divert attention in some pleasant way
OED, 1971

Prefatory Remarks

This work is not intended as salacious literature but rather as a reference for those seeking guidance upon the art of seducing men into your service. Unlike most works on the subject of sexual domination within relationships, this one does not deal with pain, humiliation, and abuse. I encourage fair, open, and honest communication between consenting mature adults. I also encourage these same adults, since all true relationships are those between equals; do not play *a la séductrice* always, but to use this style of play as a treat—something special between you and him.

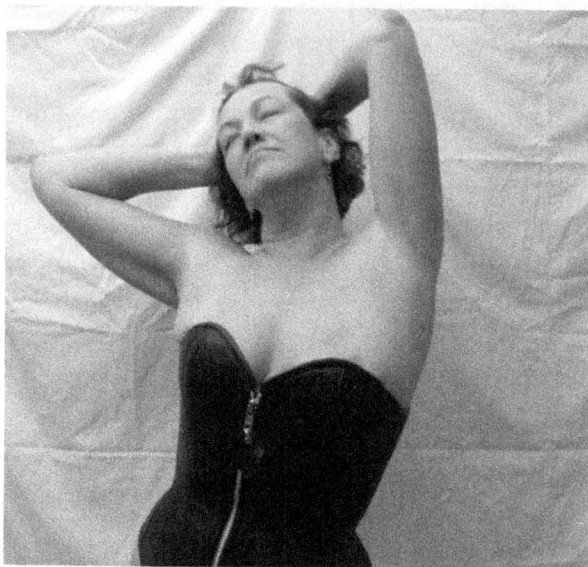

by Camden C. Cochran

We have all seen them; confident women who seem to effortlessly draw men to them and who seem to enjoy their company without taking men too seriously. Poised women dressed well, mildly flirting with men, and seemingly enjoying life in general. Chances are, that woman is a domme. She may appear nice to you but the men looking into her eyes are not deceived. They know what she is and most will find her intriguing and very, very seductive. A domme represents forbidden territory to most men. She is something different, something new, and something intoxicating. We all are aware of how attractive "forbidden fruit" is. For him, she is Cleopatra wrought anew, attended by all the allure of a not-so-silken dalliance.

She also tends to strike fear in men's hearts. A multi-orgasmic, sexually awake, and entirely self-aware woman can be very intimidating. This is not what we wish to do. Our aim is to acquire all of the allure and none of the fear.

Dommes are not glamorous, but they are not cute either. They do not go out into the world wielding whips and wearing thigh-high boots. Forget the stereotypes. You do not need a completely new wardrobe. You do not need to play "dress-up" either. The dommes I know wear sheath dresses with high-heeled pumps and look very much like any other stockbroker. It is not the costume that matters, it is all about attitude. You can learn this.

Developing the "command attitude" is very easy. You simply have to accept the concept that you are in control and in charge. Mind you that being in charge also means being responsible. There are a few rules you must learn before you begin. The first is that you never dominate anyone who is unwilling. They must consent. Going along with the idea constitutes consent. If at any time they decide not to continue, you must stop. Next, you must not leave anyone tied up for more than 45 minutes at any one time. It is bad for them. Finally, you must never ever tie him up and leave the room. Violating any of these rules is a serious error because you are putting him in harm's way. You must always remember that you are dealing with another human being and that you are totally responsible for his welfare. Do not make your play into a nightmare that will haunt him and taint any relationships he may have afterward. We are only here for fun.

This is why I do not use whips. I like my men, and I respect them since it takes courage to hand over control to another. Therefore, I do not ask them to do anything dangerous or distasteful. I am assuming that you care for your man or men as well. This is all about pleasure and fantasies; nothing more.

I did say men. Yes, "playing the field" is not only permitted, it is encouraged. If you are in a committed monogamous relationship that is one thing, but if you are not, you can enjoy as many men as you wish. Many women have a primary relationship with several additional male friends, that is to say, they are polyamorous. However you choose to arrange your life and define your relationships is fine. Nevertheless, if you are sexually active especially with multiple partners, please be sure to practice safe sex. Use both birth control and condoms. If he does not have a condom, then there is no sex. About this, there is no debate. Yes, we understand all about sensation but it is not worth dying for.

Preliminaries

The fine art of seducing men begins within yourself. You must be completely comfortable with who you are and what you are before you begin. Too many women retain erroneous notions regarding sex and relationships with men from their childhood. They have developed habits more suitable for homemakers than for lovers. This is fine except when one begins teaching him to knit instead of kissing him. We were all taught how to be "good girls" instead of women. When you decide to join the ranks of beguiling dommes (dominatrices), you have to change how you have learned to regard men.

Men are not the all-powerful ravening beasts to whom a woman must say no as often as possible. Withholding sex from him as some sort of reward for good behavior should not be done except within the context of "play." You have to come to see men for what they really are—just people who think a little differently than you do and who have a very hard time keeping up with a fully self-aware woman's sex drive. Ah, a new perspective! You are the ravening beast now. Many women are not only unaware that they have a sex drive; many have not yet had an orgasm. Now is the time to become aware of exactly what you are capable of sexually. Women can enjoy multiple orgasms, rolling orgasms, aftershocks, and yes, they do also ejaculate.

Experimenting with sex is very educational, and I encourage you to begin your machinations as soon as may be possible. According to the book of "good girls", flirting, that is using charm to manipulate men, is bad. Nonsense! Flirting is a delightful game that men enjoy playing as much as you do. Then there is that word, manipulating. Women have been castigated as being "manipulating" seemingly forever. May I remind you that politics was not invented yesterday and that Machiavelli was a man? Charm is one of your greatest weapons, and subtle flirting is the means by which you deploy that weapon.

The major stumbling block for many women is their internal body image—the "I'm too fat syndrome". Whatever shape you are is just fine unless it negatively impacts your health. Men are not nearly as picky as you might think. The vast majority are elated that you notice them at all. The idea that you might possibly want a closer relationship with them, even indulge in sexual activity with them, sends them into exultation! All that is really required is a change in attitude. Individual men may prefer blondes over brunettes or vice versa, but men in general are willing to play with whoever invites them.

Men are not "naturally dominant" and women are not "naturally submissive." Humans are much too variable for such simple definitions. Even dominant men relish the opportunity for a vacation from having to make decisions now and again. Powerful, successful men are, many times, a professional domme's best clients. If you think your man will not go for it, you might be very pleasantly surprised. You have nothing to lose and all to gain. There is not just one kind of masculinity or of femininity.

Now to begin, you do not need a lot of equipment. Since I do not advocate the use of whips and so on, your costs are minimal. A basic kit would usually include a collar and leash both of which can be bought innocently enough at any pet store in the large dog section. Candles and massage oils are readily available at the grocery store. All that remains is for you to make sure that your time this evening will not be interrupted. If you would like some ideas on how to begin, several scenarios have been included in the back of the book.

Males are usually interested in sex. A woman willing to play rarely meets with a refusal. However, since it does happen, you will have to learn how to deal gracefully with rejection. It also happens that a man may not be able to get or sustain an erection. It does happen and it is very demoralizing for a man. Being kind to him in both situations yields great benefits to a beguiling domme. By being kind and understanding (snuggling is good here), you bind him to you almost as much as you would with sexual intercourse. Remember that this is not the Olympics, and no one is keeping score. Besides, he can do other things for you. Cunnilingus and using his hands effectively will also work. In either case, his satisfaction will come from pleasing you. Do not be hesitant to tell him what you enjoy and how you want it done. Each woman has her own style, and men are accommodating when it comes to sex. Expressions of delight work better than those of discontent.

In the beginning of any sexual relationship, men will try a medley of techniques that he has learned to find just the right touch and the right degree of pressure to use for you. This is why I recommend sexually experienced men who have not been sexually compliant before. He should have some basic skills before he begins learning to play in this style, otherwise the learning curve is too steep and too fast. He will find it all overwhelming rather than pleasurable.

The education is also mutual. Both of you will discover his likes and dislikes. Men spend so much of their lives focused upon finding, getting, pleasing, and keeping women that they have little time or energy left to consider themselves. Exploring him while he remains passive beneath your hands, teeth, lips, and fingernails is an excellent way to find just what he enjoys and how he likes it. Caressing, massaging everywhere but "there" can drive a man crazy with desire. You know this, of course. However, had you realized that he would, literally, beg for it as well? You may grant his desires as you wish, but I recommend keeping the pleasure mutual.

It has been determined that a man's heart is improved by three full sexual experiences per week. Although women were not included in this study, one can reasonably infer that women also similarly benefit. Sex is good for people. Rather than the "two minute quickie" sort of sex, this style of play prolongs the pleasure into a mutually satisfying, elaborate, mingling dance taking place over a 2- to 4-hour period.

Sadly, as we go through life, we develop habits. Parents spend so much time working, raising kids, looking after the house and so on, that we get into the habit of just falling into bed, kissing goodnight, and rolling over to go to sleep. Business owners spend time going over the books. And the "über" rich rarely spend any time together at all. You have to include time for sex with your partner in your life. Make sex play your next "bad habit."

Humans find symbols very powerful. Certain archetypes are deeply rooted in our brains. This is why symbols matter. And this is why the collar is a necessary piece of equipment. Wearing a collar has a profound psychological impact upon a person and especially on a man. When fitting it, you must be able to slide three fingers between the collar and his neck. A tag is optional. Do not get some-thing slender and delicate when selecting a collar for him. Men look best in collars more suitable for rottweilers and mastiffs than they do in collars that are more delicate. It is a question of proportion. Besides, you do not want to insult the man by equating him to a chihuahua. There are men who can wear a collar and leash with a great deal of panache. I have seen this. He was wearing only a "bad boy" grin and sitting on my sofa at the time. I found the sight very attractive.

Leashes are very useful as they can be looped over bed corners and so on, as well as attached directly to the collar. Cuffs serve as both restraints and as symbols. Farther along, just putting one cuff on one wrist is enough to signal playtime to him. For a more interactive style of play, you may consider using a half-diagonal restraining arrangement where his right wrist and his left ankle are cuffed and tied to the bed, leaving the others free so he can participate as well as receive.

Humans are very visually oriented, men especially so. Blindfolding takes the visual away. This has the effect of heightening the other senses as he strives to replace the visual input. He feels more when you caress him when he cannot see you. Being blind also increases his anticipation since he cannot see your approach and thus guess your intentions. This effect is increased even further when you ask him to be active instead of just lying there and taking it. He has to use other means to find his way.

After collar, leashes, and cuffs, a blindfold should be you next addition to your play kit.

Time for a digression. Human anatomy has made us somewhat unique in that we have organs specifically designed for pleasure during sexual inter-course. Men and women both have G-spots. But there is not a great deal of room down there so these g-spots have to be tucked in somewhere. In women, it is in the top of her vagina at the base of her clitoris. In men, it is next to their prostate gland and is reached through his rectum. Yes, I know. But, sometimes sex is messy. In any case, caressing of the G-spot during sexual intercourse makes the orgasm absolutely atomic.

In the case of vibrators, there are two general types; the flat-headed clitoral stimulators and the sleeker ones meant for insertion. There are probes designed specifically for G-spot stimulation of men. They are battery powered and have variable speeds. They are also inexpensive. If you wish to try this, I recommend two "vibes" for her, clitoral and vaginal, and one probe for him. The clitoral vibrator has a flat top with small bumps on it. One word of caution, use these with care and delicacy and then keep them very clean. Only the waterproof ones, meant to be used in the shower or bath, can be run through the dishwasher. Air-drying in the sun is recommended. There are all kinds of toys available. However, this is enough for now.

> *I recommend walking around naked in your living room.*
>
> **Alanis Morissette**

A Little Anatomy

Sexual anatomy is only covered in its most basic form in school. Therefore, I will cover it here. I will not get into the hormones involved, nothing too technical here. I will also limit this to just those places of particular interest since to cover all areas that can be stimulated for sexual pleasure requires several volumes on its own. And we do not have time for all of that anyway.

In women, the clitoris, the vagina, and the G-spot are the main centers of sexual delight. Some care must be taken, as these organs tend to be specialized and sensitive. I would also like to call your attention to the Biden glands, as you will need to know about them a little later on. Much is already known about the clitoris and the vagina so we will focus upon the lesser-known G-spot and the Biden glands. Please peer closely and notice the thin red line between the vagina, below, and the bladder, above. This is the G-spot. It lies almost halfway between the cervix and the vaginal opening. Everything is densely packed and some G-spot stimulation can be achieved anally as well as vaginally. No need to be shy here, you may or may not like this sort of thing, but know that it is possible.

Towards the end of the G-spot, which is that part furthest away from the vaginal opening, lie the Biden glands. As you may be aware, a sexually interested woman "creams", that is, she releases some preparatory fluids. These are from a different set of glands. However, a woman also ejaculates, releasing a stream of carbohydrate-rich fluid. This is the "squirting" you nay have heard about. Squirting! Yes, women do "ejaculate" when they have just been blasted past Jupiter by an orgasm. First they cream, and then they squirt. It is from the Biden glands inside the vagina, and it is a fluid of complex carbohydrates (tastes sweet so I have been told) released to maintain vaginal health. A woman must be both relaxed and aroused to squirt. It is NOT a water sport and it has nothing to do with urinating. It IS a testament to a male's skill. She will not squirt all of the time or every time. A man who is clever with his hands can induce just this kind of "relaxed arousal" in his domme.

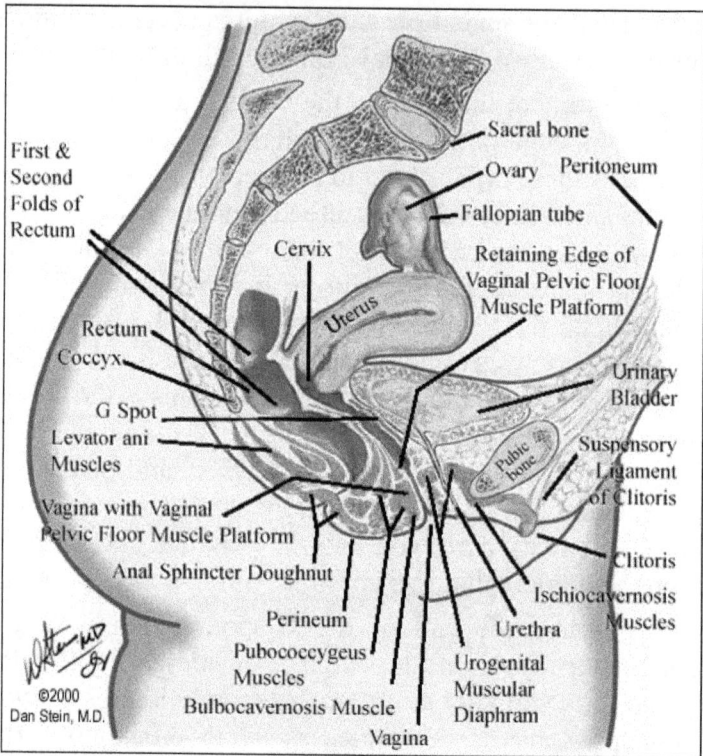

First &
Second
Folds of
Rectum

Sacral bone

Ovary Peritoneum

Fallopian tube

Cervix

Retaining Edge of
Vaginal Pelvic Floor
Muscle Platform

Uterus

Rectum

Coccyx

Urinary
Bladder

G Spot

Levator ani
Muscles

Pubic
bone

Suspensory
Ligament
of Clitoris

Vagina with Vaginal
Pelvic Floor Muscle Platform

Anal Sphincter Doughnut

Clitoris

Ischiocavernosis
Muscles

Perineum

Urethra

Pubococcygeus
Muscles

Urogenital
Muscular
Diaphram

©2000
Dan Stein, M.D.

Bulbocavernosis Muscle

Vagina

To aide in his education, I include the following information of just what he would feel during this endeavor.

The Guided Tour. *As you go in, you will find first a kind of squashed grape structure covered* *with goose bumps in the front and on the top. These goose bumps enlarge and become more prominent as her excitement mounts. Then there is a central raised area going further back with two grooves on either side. Further in, you come to a raised bar going from side to side followed by an area like a washboard. You may not reach the bar or washboard as she may be too excited to permit you to get back that far as she clamps down upon you or your hand. But if you stroke upwards gently while exploring these features, you just might get very, very wet. Yes, a man can induce squirting using his penis as well. The female ejaculate is perfectly safe to drink; although it does not do very much for his contacts if he is wearing them at the time. It does come out with some pressure and can be copious, so having towels nearby would be a good idea. The ejaculate evaporates quickly without a stain.*

Now for the man and his anatomy. Once again, we will skip lightly over the obvious and go right for his P-spot.

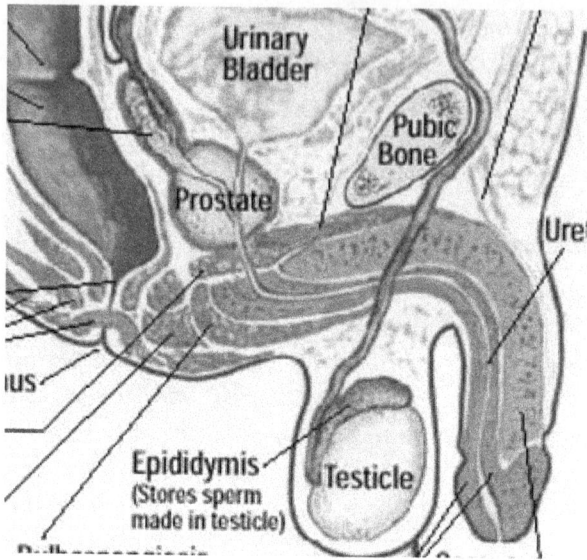

It is the back surface of the prostate that we want, the side towards the rectum. The posterior surface, the P-spot location (*facies posterior*), is flattened from side to side and slightly convex from above downward; it is separated from the rectum by its sheath and some loose connective tissue, and is distant about 4 cm from the anus.

Not a great deal of pressure or vibration is needed to enhance his orgasm, but how much varies between men, so I cannot give you specific figures. You will have to conduct experiments.

As we age, life takes its toll upon us. Being understanding will go a long way to building your relationships with your men. Erectile spongy tissues in both sexes fill with blood during arousal. Poor circulation, nerve damage, hormone imbalance and performance anxiety may cause inadequate blood flow. The erectile tissue of the clitoris is much larger than previously thought. Deteriorated spongy tissue may allow blood to leak out, sabotaging male erection or female arousal. Hardening of the arteries, high cholesterol, hypertension, diabetes, and diet can produce fatty deposits that constrict the inside diameter of genital arteries and restrict blood flow. This can also impair function of the spongy tissue. Sensory nerves may lose sensitivity with aging, low sex hormones, physical injury, or surgery. Nerve impairment may occur with diabetes, smoking, hypertension, or athletic injury. Male nerve damage may occur with surgery of the prostate, bladder, or rectum. Female nerve damage generally occurs with childbirth, hysterectomy, or surgery of the bladder or rectum. Nerve function is necessary for arousal response, ejaculation, and orgasm in both sexes.

The choices we made in our youth, such a motor-cross, will have a negative impact upon our bodies when we age. Yet, not taking risks makes for a very dull life. Being kind, gentle, and understanding is necessary to building a good relationship. One can work around physical ailments and conditions or one can deal with them medically. But they should not get in the way building and enjoying a joyous sexual relationship. Some drugs taken for medical reasons do have a negative effect upon a person's sexuality. This may require a performance enhancing drug to counteract the first drug. Alternatively, one can just accept it and move on to other methods. For example, Lipitor requires the male user to also use Viagra or Cialas in most cases. Taking Lipitor may, on the other hand, have no effect upon a person. You will just have to investigate each partner's needs individually.

You, yourself, may not the terror you once were either. Are you prepared to deal effectively with your own liabilities? Fair is fair after all. One can only ask for what one is also willing to give. Care and consideration in even the Mistress/slave relationship goes both ways. Will you permit him to care for you should you need it? Consulting appropriate medical professionals may be required.

Safe Play Practices. If the submissive says stop, the play stops. Limits are never to be tested or pushed. Dominants must earn trust, not demand it. You earn trust by being trustworthy at all times. The only proper punishment is to ignore the erring submissive. Never leave the room while play is ongoing. Do not ever leave a submissive tied up in any fashion for longer than 45 minutes at one time. If you wish to try something new and different, discuss this with the submissive beforehand and give him/her time to consider it and decide whether to participate.

There are some issues that men have to deal with before they can agree to participate in these sexual adventures. They are all bound up in being "less of a man." He does not want him to see himself as less of a man; he does not want you to see him as less than a man; and he does not want anyone else to know about it lest they see him as less than a man. To deal with the self-image issue, you will have to give him time to adjust to the idea. He has to consider the proposition; then he has to make a decision. Give him time to do both. This shows that you respect him as a person.

The fact that you want to play with him in this way indicates you want a closer relationship. He has to come to grips with both concepts and decide what it all means to him.

You must respect his decision be it yeah or nay. If he decides not to play this way, then you have to decide whether to continue the relationship as it is now or to move on to another one entirely. In many ways, it is a trust issue. Can he trust you? Can he trust himself? Is he emotionally strong enough to sexually submit to you? Is he confident enough in his masculinity to sexually submit to you? These are questions that only he can answer. Deciding while in a "what the hell" kind of mood or in drunken moment is not the kind of consideration needed. However, trying it once will give him more information upon which to base his decision. Let us suppose that he does agree to submit sexually. Will you see him as being less of a man for it? Intellectually considering the topic is not enough, you have to experience it and then decide if you still respect him. Open and honest communication after playing once will help and bring hidden concerns to the surface. You both can then address these issues and deal with them as mature adults who happen to like each other. Please do not focus upon the semantics of the words here. This is a relationship between equals: one where each feels comfortable being who they are. This may require you both to make attitude adjustments.

Arranging her skirts, she straddled my lap facing me on my sofa. She was so beautiful. Her eyes laughed and sparkled. Her lips curved delightfully and when she kissed me so lightly all of the desire I had for her flared up. Delicately kissing my lips over and over making me quiver. When she lifted her face away I became aware of the collar around my neck. I said nothing as she began undoing my shirt buttons and running her hands through my chest hair, caressing me. I stopped her hands at my belt buckle. It was too soon for me. Yes, I wanted her. But between wanting and having lay issues. A messy past, an uncertain future, and a woman I barely knew snuggling into my arms as I wore her collar around my neck. There was that ring on her left hand. Where did that put me? Yes I wanted her, who would not? But I am not a young guy heedless of consequences. 'No, not tonight.' You know I was kicking myself as I went upstairs to bed after watching her drive off.

What I wanted was not what she could give.
What I wanted, she already had. Where did that
leave me? Yes, she's a domme but I haven't seen a
whip yet. She seems kind and patient. I like her as a
person, and I care about her as a friend. What am I
getting myself into? She wants me? A beautiful
woman wants me? And here I am somewhat
bewildered since I am not a young tall hard-bodied
hunk who's hung like a horse. I am not bad, but she
could have any man she really wanted. I am not rich
either. She must just like me for some reason. What
do I know about women? I tried to resist, but then
she was sitting next to me on my sofa. She had my
shirt off and she ran her fingertips slowly and lightly
up my spine, blew gently on the nape of my neck,
and lightly licked my ear. Okay, okay, I give in!
Take me upstairs to my bed! She did. I did. We did.

Still no whips. She doesn't need them. Force of
personality, drop dead sexy beauty, razor
intelligence, and a skill at seduction that you have
to experience to believe makes coercion
unnecessary. Yeah, I am her slut.

It is not necessary for you to go public or to turn your
life around into some grand lifestyle complete with all of
the trap-pings and philosophies. You do not need a
dungeon; your bed will do just fine. You also do not need
to document the moment on any media. You do not have to
join any clubs or networks. You know we are out here. No
new wardrobes are required. This doesn't need to be some
grand production. A nice quiet affair will work very nicely.
So if you or he should prefer to keep this to your-selves, go
right ahead.

Little things that matter
1. *being offered a man's arm when walking*
2. *contently curling up in his arms*
3. *a "pet name"*
4. *having a bathrobe available for her/his use*
5. *trusting him enough to nap with him*
6. *him making sure she is warm enough*
7. *stargazing*
8. *not fearing to touch him*
9. *her taking her shoes off*
10. *being able to be silly with him/her*

However, if you would like to venture out, here are some ideas. Your choices are: soft swap, threesomes and foursomes, and groups also known as multiples.

Safe Sex Practices. *Unless you are in committed monogamous relationship, the lady is in charge of birth control and the man must wear a condom. If you are sexually active with multiple partners, have yourself tested every six months. Wash all equipment and toys after each use. You are free to make your own choices but carrying something back is indefensible.*

Teddybears are not just furry and somewhat burly men. They have a certain attitude that I find extremely hard to resist. I simply must reach out and hug, kiss, and fuck them. Do not ask me why—it just is. Something along the lines of a confident masculinity that while they truly love women are also not blind to their flaws, their needs, and their desires. Men who can not only handle a woman throwing herself into their arms, but also know just what to do with her when they catch her. Amused, amusing, and always very, very willing to join me in whatever I might have in mind. I can spot him within moments. A warm, comfortable man that a lady can take to bed with her with complete confidence.

The Ultimate Winter Bed. Guaranteed to keep even the tenderest of ladies warm and comfortable through the night. Begin with a firm, if not rock hard, mattress and box springs, then cover this with a two to three inch featherbed.

Use 600-thread count sheets—yes, a bit pricey but they will last almost to forever, so it's worth it. On go the sheets in the usual approved manner (if you do not know – ask) If your budget cannot stand 600-thread count sheets, you may use flannel sheets.

On top of this, place what is known as a mink blanket, that is to say a double thickness, heavy-weight blanket. This will help mold the fabrics to her body, preventing cold air infiltration. Top off with a down comforter in a flannel cover; yes the heavy blanket goes under the comforter. Three firmnesses of pillows are best: rock-hard, medium, and squishy, all in 600-thread count or flannel pillowslips. You may use less if you do not have a king size bed. Why don't you have a king size bed, by the way? Never mind. To make it very special indeed, add one attractive and congenial adult male human.

Multiple and groups can be fun, but including play or incorporating play into a group setting can be fraught. Threesomes and foursomes are easier to deal with, especially for beginners. Finding others with whom to enjoy yourselves is done by contacting your local swing group. Every community has one, and then there is the internet. Just be aware of the hazards, respectful of your primary relationship, and discrete.

Two women ganging up on one man is every man's fantasy. Two men serving one woman is glorious fun. But some people have issues with sharing. Jealousy is bred of fear. Fear of losing one's man or woman to another. Fear that he or she may not be good enough somehow for you or not enough for you. You have to deal with these issues and the lack of trust and self-respect before you venture out. It is not fair to subject another person to your drama.

You can unlearn jealousy. People can learn to not compete when it comes to sex. If everyone gets along well together, there should be no problems. By calmly and quietly discussing issues with your playmates, you can overcome most of these insecurities.

Be aware that bisexuality is only an option and not a given. Incorporating play into a three or four-some is easily done. All you have to do is to slip on his collar and invite the other ladies to enjoy him. In the case of multiple men, slip all of them into collars and play with them as you wish. While tethering may be logistically difficult it can be done also. Blindfolds are easier to employ. I would suggest enjoying them in straight sex first until everyone is quite comfortable with each other before introducing play elements. That way it all becomes play between friends.

If you keep a stable of men, or a male harem if you prefer the term, it is interesting to watch them interact. They will form a social net of their own. One male was regarded as the enforcer of the rules; the man who would be in charge of protecting my person. Another was my social representative and escort. If I went out somewhere, he was the one who accompanied me. He also served as my designated driver and/or navigator as required. A third man was solely in charge of calling me at noon to remind me to eat lunch. They formed a nice little hierarchy all on their own without involving me at all. Watching it happen was very interesting.

All of this is entirely optional. I just happen to be polyamorous. As long as no one is harmed, there will be no judgments made. Where you will run into trouble, is if you select the wrong person or persons to join you, so be very careful to interview people beforehand. Do this together. Exchange notes afterwards and discuss every candidate. You may want to include a test date as part of your selection process.

If you have children at home, I strongly encourage you to not introduce this person to your family or to your home until you are utterly and completely assured of their suitability and reliability. While I have never been stalked—few dommes are, it is too dangerous—I do have a female vanilla friend who was. She did not find it a pleasant experience. A network of friends—both male and female—is one's best protection against this sort of thing, especially if one includes various professions within this network. Proper documentation and the correct use of both law enforcement and the legal profession will remedy this sort of thing.

Once you have decided the guest list, the next item is to arrange a venue. Hotel suites are excellent choices if your budget will allow for one. You do not want your life taken over by this, so if one of your guests has a suitable place, then I suggest you ask if they would care to host it there. Of course, we all pay for our pleasures, but some charges are simply ridiculous, and a private residence is usually much more comfortable. Just be careful not to trespass upon their privacy more often than is seemly.

The same rules apply as they would at any house party. It is just that at these, the people wear fewer clothes and generally indulge in more intimate pleasures. Safe sex practices are a must, and the thoughtful host places bowls containing variously sized unopened condoms about where they might be needed. Fancy bathrobes are a nice touch as well. It might get chilly out by the swimming pool or on the deck. Alcohol to excess and any drugs are not to be indulged in. Play can be dangerous to some people and everyone must be in full control of their faculties to remain safe. Smoking is done outside unless told otherwise.

Requests for play are gently made and their acceptance or refusal is received with grace. If you must decline an invitation do so with kindness. Try not to leave anyone out. All of the guests should be friends with whom you would like to spend some time. When play is incorporated there is a slight change in the rules. You do not speak to slaves directly. You must go through their domme. In all of this, please be aware of your man's feelings. If he feels uncomfortable or upset, deftly seek him out and find out why. Since he is yours, you are the responsible party. Whether naked or clothed, Mistress or slaves, the rules of social engagement remain those of Miss Manners. You also have your primary relationship to maintain.

How to Setup Group Activities

1. *Announce it, including any special arrangements (such as BYOC "bring your own condom" or BYOB "bring your own booze") and if they have to ante up for the room, and collect couples, men, and extra women as desired*

2. *Get first names, email addresses, and cell numbers—you email the invitations.*

3. *Invite twice as many men as women as not all will actually come.*

4. *Double check several days beforehand to make certain that all is well.*

5. *On the day, call all to tell them which room.*

6. *After the party, when it is just you and your primary, shower together and chat.*

Being asked by a participating lady to share the shower with her is a privilege. Take care to make sure her hair is dry and her back is well scrubbed.

Male Partner Selection

For those who do not yet have a partner, here are some tips to use when you set out to find one.

Other than appealing to you to the point where you are wondering how his hands and lips would feel on your skin, you have to carefully consider several other criteria when selecting a male slut or when selecting a male to turn into a slut.

1. Can he get his mind around the concept of any woman, at any time he is required, anyway she wants him? Can he be passed around amongst the ladies like a six-pack? Would he enjoy it?

2. Does he have the *cajones* to submit without being obsequious or fawning? You want a man not a dog after all.

3. Is he presentable? If all you wanted was a penis, you could go buy one. Can he converse and how are his manners?

4. Is he willing to learn and open to new ideas and experiences?

5. Does he genuinely like women? You know what I mean by that—and yes, we can tell if he does.

Now all we have to consider is his amount of available free time, transport, and wherewithal (since you do not want to end up having to support him). Self-sufficient but willing men with the necessary free time are what you want. If he volunteers, that's even better!

Once you have found him, and he has agreed to play, you then have to train him. The following lessons are pleasant for you both. One lesson per week is about the right frequency. Mingle the lessons in among your regular scheduled sex periods.

Male Slut Lesson #1

Having selected your male slut, it now is time to train him. This is classic on-the-job training, so make sure you have all of the necessary devices and implements ready and at hand. All training is done on a positive basis: good boys get rewarded, bad boys get ignored. The object of this lesson is to reinforce the idea of ownership/possession. He is yours.

Have him get naked and then kneel before you. Put the collar around his neck, the individual unlinked cuffs on his wrists and attach the leash to the collar.

Provocatively and sensually caress him all over his body ignoring any erections at first. He is not to orgasm just yet. Take your time and become very familiar with his body, his hot buttons, his tickle spots, etc.

With him still kneeling, sit down before him and have him undo the buttons on your shirt. He is do exactly what you tell him to do, as you want it done, and to keep on doing it until you tell him to stop.

Work from your chest down-ward. Permit him access as you wish. Then you lie down and have him do body worship with hands and mouth. Have him take his time. Be sure to provide plenty of direction so he learns how best to please you. Have as many orgasms as you like but do not permit him to have any…yet.

When you are fully satiated, it is now time to reward him for his diligence. I recommend having him masturbate for you so you can study his preferred style of manipulation. Mind that you do not touch him in any way. You can provide verbal and/or visual stimulation should you desire to do so. But do not touch him. Afterwards, providing him with a warmed wet washcloth and a hug would be nice. Keep it friendly. Here ends the lesson.

NOTES:

Male Slut Lesson #2

To continue with the training program, and in addition to the items previously used, you will need a vibrating anal probe. Do not get excited and move too fast, as most males are timid when you start wielding vibrators around them. The point of this lesson is to firmly fix in his mind the idea that his pleasure comes from you and that he is to accept what you have in mind for him.

He is beginning to trust you. Once again he is suitably attired in his leather accessories. Have him perform cunnilingus for you. Then, place him on his stomach on the bed. Your attitude is that he is your prey. You begin caressing him all over slowly using hands, mouth, and body while purring over this delicious "catch" of yours. Ignore his genitals for now. Enjoy yourself immensely while doing this too. He is not permitted to move at all.

Have him roll over and then repeat on the front side; also ignoring his genitals. He still cannot move. By this time he should be ready for what comes next.

Lube up your hand(s) and start caressing his penis. Use additional lube as is necessary. After a short time, start the vibe where he cannot see it and apply it just behind his testicles and gently press it there while continuing to caress him to orgasm and ejaculation.

Once again, hand him a warm wet washcloth and give him a hug. He should thank you after each lesson. Here ends the lesson.

You may wish to spend some time alternating between lessons 1 and 2. Or you may be combine this lesson with lesson 1. If he has been particularly good, you may wish to reward his excellent service by indulging in lesson 2 again.

NOTES:

Male Slut Lesson #3

Now that he has had some basic training, you can begin to establish some patterns of behavior and develop his trust. This time he will have his wrist cuffs attached together, making his hands unavailable. Should you also wish him to wear a blindfold, now would be a good time to introduce him to one.

Remember when creating your plans for him that you get your pleasure before he gets his reward. You must be consistent upon this one item more than any other. He must please you. If he does not, for whatever reason, you must immediately leave his side and pretend he does not exist for a short period of time. You will, of course, not leave the room and will occupy yourself with various activities that will generate some small noise so he knows you are there. Say some-thing like "5 minutes," and be sure you return to him in five minutes. He has to know he can rely upon you.

Help him arrange himself for kneeling cunnilingus and have him perform to your complete satisfaction. Then you have you choice of arranging him onto the bed and tying him so as to allow for various sexual configurations.

This is the first time he gets his chance to perform actual coitus. Unless he has presented current medical evidence of being disease free, use a condom. If you have any doubts, use a condom.

I recommend that he be the static partner; immobile while you take your pleasure using his body as your instrument. Using the minimal of equipment, this would mean attaching his collar to one end of the leash/rope and his cuffs to the other end and looping the leash/rope around a bedpost or leg. He is then on his back and you are in the female superior position.

The reason for depriving him the use of his hands and/or eyes is to force him to feel more—use his remaining senses to make up for the lack of touch and sight, this increases his sensitivity and appreciation when he gets their use back.

Slowly release him, cuddle, and then clean up! Here ends the lesson.

NOTES:

These next two lessons may be hard for you since they involve sharing your man with other women. If you feel that you cannot, never mind. It is always your choice.

Male Slut Lesson #4

We now move into the final stages of the male slut's formal training. He regards his nakedness, his accessories, and his kneeling postures as normal. He assumes them all with calm and a degree of happiness. During his training, he only receives his rewards when suitably attired. Since his role is going to be "please every woman who wants him," he must be trained in the various techniques he will need to fulfill his role. For this training, you will need additional women. I hope you have some friends. You give your male over to her for training in what she prefers but you are responsible for his performance. Any failures mean he will have to be drilled on that particular area until he can perform reliably at the desired level of skill. You will remain there to supervise, of course.

Each lady must be willing to provide direction, correction, and recommendations. Remember to praise in public but to reprimand and criticize only in private. Naturally, you want your male able and willing to perform with every woman, so you will provide him with a variety of women as associate trainers. Whether he finds her attractive and desirable is not important. He has to understand this.

The women must be willing to use him in a manner consistent with your training, so the use of hard dommes who specialize in humiliation, pain, and abuse, etc. would not be suitable.

You also want your male slut to be socially presentable. Should a lady require a male to escort her to some social function, you would volunteer him for the job.

The more outings you send him on, the better. If you participate in sex parties, you will want him to attend you, but he will not participate without your express permission. Take him shopping. Take him to the zoo for the afternoon, anything will do. Once you begin taking him out in public, he may dispense with his accessories. In private sessions, you will want to expand his experiences such as finding his G-spot, various threesomes and foursomes, some vertical work, etc.

Often you will find that his greatest problem will be being in the same room with another naked man or men. If he focuses closely upon his job, he should get over that quickly.

There is an etiquette to such adventures and he will need to learn it if he is to join in the fun. One hard and fast rule is the use of condoms. He must use them. In any case, end the evening alone together with some discussion and some hugs. Many enjoy this stage so much that they do not ever leave it. There is no time frame attached to this stage. Here ends the lesson.

NOTES:

Male Slut Lesson #5

This is the final step in your male slut's training. By now, he should be ready to fulfill any lady's desires. This lesson adds one final element based upon the realities of life. He has learned that he can trust you, now you have to learn to trust him. You are having him attend you on various excursions. The difference now is that he will be participating. You have to let some of the control over him go.

Your friends know that he is available to him and they should be calling for him. During girl chats, you freely offer him up to them by firmly stating that you share. Beyond generally being civil, you do not ask for particulars of how it went. The time for that has passed. You do not ask and he does not tell. You have already witnessed him with other women; now he is servicing them without you being there. Can you stand it? Naturally, he will continue to spend time with you and will continue in your service. Group play and house parties form a regular social pattern for you both. But when you play singly, there is no discussion.

The lesson here is for you to let him go and for him to not forget his primary obligation. Has the "freedom" gone to his head? What if he forms a lasting emotional bond with another? This, and similar, situations can be difficult for you both. You may find that his time for you is less than you would like. If you bring on another male slut, how will this affect your relationship with him?

What you will find is that once you two have worked out this phase of your relationship, you both no longer need those leather accessories and the restraints—oh, you may get them out upon occasion just for fun, but you both can be more relaxed about it. Just be sure to incorporate what you have learned over the course of the lessons into your regular sexual encounters. Mutual sexual satisfaction is the key here. Here ends the lesson.

NOTES:

You may find over time that he may want more from you than you would care to give. Perhaps his experiences with other women have moved him further along than you require or desire him to be. If this is the case, you may want to hand him over to another lady and find another primary for yourself.

Do not totally separate yourself from him. You should retain some access to him and his services as one of your interlocking intimate relationships. So long as there is mutual consent among all parties, there is no real reason to completely end any relationship. Polyamory is a wonderful way to live. But since polyamorous relationships can get complicated, you may decide to limit yourself to just the one relationship.

So long as you can fairly divide your time, you will find that you can have a few male sluts should you wish to. You will end up with a group of ladies who share a cadre of willing and able men, which is a very comfortable arrangement.

Should you choose to be polyamorous, be aware that not everyone will be receptive or willing to accept you. Society tends to have a somewhat elevated idea of the value of the pair bond. Should marriage arise, the situation can become even more fraught and complex. Children add both joy and difficulties. As long as everyone behaves as a reasonable, rational, and compassionate adult, these difficulties can be overcome.

Jealousy is not a given. We learn to be jealous. We are taught to be jealous. It is nonsense. Each of us is capable of loving many people both singularly in series or simultaneously. If he is out with someone else, no matter, you will survive.

If you have limits, please discuss them beforehand. You rule your household, of course, but each of us has her/his issues, and these must be dealt with if you are going to live a happy fulfilled life. In my case, it is my bed. No other women are permitted in my bed. Other than this, I have no anxieties. At parties, I will share bed space with other women and men—the rule only applies to my own personal bed.

Take the time before a situation arises to wrap your mind around the concept and investigate your emotions and thoughts on the subject. For example, how do you feel about your male being or becoming bi-curious or bi-sexual? Would you ask him to perform bisexually with you and another male? Female bisexuality is far more easily accepted than male bisexuality; especially by men and dommes. Even men who appreciate a domme's use of a strap-on on them may well balk at the idea of accepting another male in that role. As the person in charge, it is your responsibility to consider these issues.

You find, as one friend of mine did, that you enjoy watching two men play with each other, only to find out that when the men really get into it, that you begin feeling neglected and have to take your proper place in between them. But this often happens with threesomes, especially with couples if you are the "third."

Children are never permitted to witness anything in the way of play. Public displays of affection, hugging, kissing, holding hands and so forth are, of course, permitted. But play, in particular power play, should never take place near them. They should neither witness nor participate. So long as they are loved, children are very adaptable and will accept your life and your relationships. They understand the concept of friendship and this is how you would present your relationships to you children, as adult friendships.

There are a few legal ramifications of which you should be aware, such as not leaving anyone tied up alone and not letting anyone remain tied up for more than 45 minutes.

If you are not married or a blood relation, then medical issues may arise that require intervention by a doctor or hospitalization. You will not be permitted to know anything nor will you be permitted to visit or have any say in treatment. Inheritance and other legal issues, just as with same sex couples, can ruin your plans as well. I strongly suggest that you consult an attorney before entering into any financial, medical, or business arrangements with any of your men.

If their blood relations are not well disposed towards his life or to you, you may also run into problems. If there are ex-spouses about, or children and custody issues, how you live may have a disastrous effect on their resolution by judges or other third-party decision makers. Discuss these issues beforehand with your men and consult an attorney to make sure that the outcome you desire is the one that will prevail should it come to a fight.

It may seem odd, but you should also have escape clauses built into anything you arrange with your attorney should your relationship with your men deteriorate. Should you break up, the last thing you would want is a public battle in the courts.

This brings up another point. I am not a professional domme. I have no intention of ever being a professional domme and therefore do not ever hold myself out to be one. You have to be very careful about this because if a charge of prostitution can be made, it will be made. Your motivations should be clearly stated beforehand. You should also specify in any legally binding arrangements just why you are doing this. Consult with your attorney over the exact wording and intent so as to make your position and motives clear. Remember that society does not like you and will not accept you even if they fantasize about you. Protect yourself.

Protect your privacy as well. You are your first line of defense. If you do not tell them, they may guess, but they will not know. If you do not want to answer a question, do not answer it. The lack of evidence is very often a good thing. No pictures and no videos with the participants clearly identifiable are good, but not taking them in the first place is even better. You never know where they might end up. Since you are a sensible woman, you would not want to be that position.

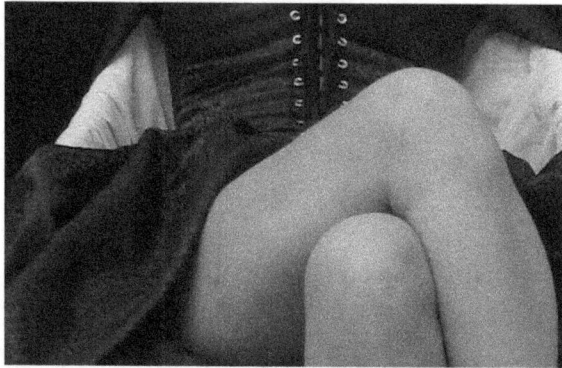

by Camden C. Cochran

Now, on to a few scenarios. You may wish to add a few of your own or modify these presented here.

I love the heat. The warmth against my skin eases me into a relaxed state where everything becomes possible. Sunlight on my flesh, hot swirling water surrounding me, the heat of a lusty man as he wraps his arms around me, I love it all. Come closer, darling. Bring those heavy muscles over here. Oh yes, just like that. Ummm, love your kiss, baby. Now slowly slide those lips down the center of my chest. That's right. Slowly down over my belly. Your hands caressing down my back to my haunches feel as hot as your mouth. Sweet Jesus! I cum into your open mouth as my orgasm screams through every sinew and synapse. I am glowing like the sun and radiating lust like plutonium. Wrapping one arm around your waist and my other hand on the back of your neck I pull you down on top of me as I lay down onto the bed behind me. The haste with which you put on your condom is endearing. I am writhing even before you enter me. Hold on tight. You've barely entered and I am cumming again! That sublime moment! Ah! You cradle my shoulders in your arms and kiss me as we move together, driving into each other. Feels so good! I wrap my legs around your hips and my nails run down your back as the next orgasm annihilates time and space. My obvious enjoyment has had its effect on you. I grin as I increase the pace. Come on, baby. Cum for me. Let me hear you! I feel so warm and wet around your cock. I lightly caress the back of your neck even as my hips powerfully roll against you. Sing for me! Oh yes! I want it! Then it comes. I hear you cry out, and I see you cum as I blink your sweat from my eyes, but I don't stop moving just yet. Double it, baby! Just one more! You barely believe it as another orgasm catches you unprepared. Yes! We lie there together beneath the sheet I pulled up over us, remembering how to breathe. Thank you, baby! is what you remember hearing as I snuggle up against you for your warmth.

The lights and heavy metal music are low as I straddle you slowly as you sit on the sofa. As I kiss your lips, I slide a black leather collar around your neck and close the buckle. You are mine now. I unbutton my shirt, directing your attention to my breasts, which you gratefully receive into your mouth. Oh, yes! "You have entirely too many clothes on baby," I breathe into his ear. I get up and we both begin a somewhat hurried strip. We won't make it up the stairs to the bed.

I wrap myself around you as we fall back onto your sofa. You are so pretty. With your mouth on my nipple, your hand seeks out my G-spot, and you have me coming in seconds! You have to lean on me, using your weight to hold me down. Yes! I must have you! I tug urgently on your collar! "Come here, baby." You slide your thick penis into me slowly. Aaaah! It feels so very, very good! Hold still as I grind against you forcing you even deeper into me. So wet and warm around you.

The feeling when a man first enters you is exquisite. I take a moment to savor the feeling. With your lips against my neck, you can feel me purr beneath you. Slowly matching the beat shaking the foundation, I wrap my arms around your torso and begin riding you from the bottom. My skin flushes as I reach orgasm. Somehow you find another gear and throw me into an even more volcanic orgasm. I cry out and writhe vigorously even as you too cum. I think to myself as I nuzzle against your furry chest, "Oh, yeah! I will keep you."

"What was your name again, baby?"

I whisper in your ear as the blindfold goes around your head, "You trust me, don't' you, baby?" "Yes, Ma'am, I do," you whisper back. We are standing in my home office; you naked before me. I just adore your muscles and the fur that lightly covers them. "Hmmmm, you look so very tasty," I purr at you while I kiss the side of your neck. I cuff your wrists together and slip the connecting chain over a hook in the ceiling. You can stand easily yet your hands are out of the way. Now I can do with you whatever I will. We haven't been together for some time, so you are already excited. Your penis is erect and aching—begging for me. Not yet. Not yet. I move around you caressing all but your penis and testicles with the articles of clothing I remove from myself, ending up facing your back. "Ready, baby?" "Yes."

"What do you say?" "Please." My claws slowly rake down your shoulders, your back, and over your rump—deep enough to be felt but not so deep as to leave marks. Ah! The pleasure you feel! Gently, I soothe your skin with my hands. "Shhh, baby, shhh," I whisper to you. Standing behind you, I gently caress up the front of your thighs and onto your hips as I press up close against your back. You can feel me, naked from the waist up, against you. My right cheek rests against your left shoulder as I continue to stroke your thighs, hips, and tummy. With agonizing slowness, I gently lick up the back of your neck and blow a gentle stream of air across it to help the moisture evaporate. I both see and feel you quiver. So very delightful. Pre-cum has formed on the head of your penis. You begin whispering over and over again: "Please, fuck me." Begging me to touch your penis. Begging me to relieve your lust. Not yet.

Not yet. I kiss you gently and trace your lips with the tip of my tongue as I caress your breasts and nipples. The final bits of silk undies slide over them on their way to the floor. Then I gently claw and pinch your now hard nipples. "Do you want me, baby?" I whisper to you. "Oh, yes, please," you exhale back. I lick up the front of your neck from sternum to chin and kiss your lips again. I press my now naked body against you, your penis between us. You are sweating with the effort needed to control yourself. You have to keep from cumming for as long as is possible. You have begun to pant as I continue to circle and caress you with hands, lips, tongue, and claws. "Please fuck me." You are getting louder and more insistent. "Shhh, baby, shhh," I whisper back. You must learn to relax and enjoy the attention your mistress gives you. Learn to relish the agony of your desire. Feel the lust overwhelming your brain, flooding out all thoughts. You can smell my special perfume. It only adds to your frustration. You are almost weeping at being kept waiting for so very, very long.

"Now," I quietly say as I take firm hold of your penis with my right hand and your testicles in my left. Your orgasm comes crashing through you, from the center of the earth it seems as you throw your head back and cry out. Your cum gushing up onto your belly. Your body shakes as your senses are overloaded. You cannot see, you cannot hear, you cannot remember your own name. Yes, baby, cum for me. I want all of it. Hang there exhausted, empty, and unable to stand, with your sperm covering your belly. So very pretty. "What do you say, baby?" "Thank you, Ma'am."

began with one man in the back bedroom, on my hands and knees as he worked his penis in my vagina. Wow, he was good! I began gushing all over him. Another man was seated at the foot of the bed to my right, receiving a blow-job from a kneeling blonde. He lay back on the bed, and I began kissing his lips. I began cumming. A half-dressed couple came in and sat at the top of the bed with their back against the headboard, just watching the action. A fourth man came in and began undressing. My man came and offered his place up to the newcomer, Bob, who readily accepted. The blowjob couple had left. So my original man then asked the half-dressed lady for some. She lay down perpendicular to me, and he entered her missionary style. My original man and I began kissing, and she began kissing and biting my nipples and fondling my breasts even as the newcomer fucked me from behind. It all felt so damn good! My orgasms were rolling! I began pushing back against Bob writhing and forcing my hips back, driving his penis further up inside me! The sight of a woman totally unleashed was too much for Bob. He could not hold back any longer and came like a locomotive. We were very noisy about it.

I wandered over to the other bedroom to check on the action there but there was little room. Both beds were being used by various couples. So I wandered back to the first bedroom and, finding a man unoccupied, I enticed him onto the bed with me. And so it went throughout the evening. A man here and another man there. There were 15 men from whom I could choose.

By this time, my appetite remained unslaked and I prowled, growling, for men I had not yet enjoyed. Mark, the 30-year old, and another man were my next group. Mark bit my left nipple and used three fingers to massage my G-spot while the 30-year old, shocked to his core, bit my right nipple while I was on my back, giving the third man a blowjob. My orgasms once again rolled and the bed beneath us became drenched. I kissed Mark and gave him a hug before getting onto my hands and knees. The man, to whom I had given the blowjob, not wanting to miss the moment, quickly entered me from behind. Once again I pressed back into him, writhing, and rolling my hips forcing more orgasms. Another couple sharing the same bed was similarly engaged. The lady of that pair kissed my lips briefly and then was overtaken by her own orgasms.

A break was in order so I wandered onto the balcony. Dave followed. His interest was very evident, so back into the first bedroom we went. He was nice and thick. Ah! There's nothing quite as sweet as a man! My orgasms were harder than ever! After him came Marty. He was very compliant and went down on me. Using mouth and hands he brought me to more orgasms.

I was in the second bedroom about to enjoy yet another man, when the police knocked on the door. We all quietly got dressed and stood in the depths of the rooms until the police had left. By this time, the mood had been broken and we all slowly dispersed. There had been a total of 16 men present; of that 16, I had enjoyed or sampled 14 that night. Then I went back with my slut to his place and enjoyed him there. I think I have found my limit; 15 men in 4 hours.

I love the way you respond to slow caresses; to being touched by my hands and lips. Up along your arms, over your shoulders, sliding across your jaw and cheek, down your back, and over your thighs and rump, finishing with the lightest of lingering kisses on your lips. I give as good as I get. I want your entire body to sing. I want you blood to soar. I want your very soul to disintegrate in passion.

The sight of your naked body excites me; all of that lovely fur for me to nuzzle. I put my arms around you and kiss the side of your neck, breathe in your scent, delicious, and purr in your ear. You like my warm breath against your neck, don't you, darling. Your eyes close and your legs part as I reach down to very slowly slide the vibrating probe up your ass. Feels good, doesn't it, sweetheart. I caress your penis, feeling it hardening beneath my touch. But no, you cannot cum just yet. You stand there as I kneel down to suck your penis just enough to get the vibrating cock ring around it; easing it around your thicknesses. You have such a pretty penis.

I sit and relax watching you feel the vibrations from my toys. Then you kneel before me as I spread my legs for you. With my hands in your hair, you bend to lick and pay homage to me. "Such a sweet slut," I whisper to you as you kneel there, your tongue very busy on my clit. Oh yes, you are so very good with your mouth. I love the way the back of your shoulders look when you are kneeling before me; very tasty with all of those muscles. I run my hands slowly over those shoulders enjoying the feel of your skin.

I press the controls and send pulses to the vibrating cock ring. Your quivering responses are very seductive. "Mmmmmm, you are very, very good." You eagerly drink up my very wet orgasm. Your muffled groans of pleasure arouse me even more. Rolling orgasms run through me and the heavens turn inside out. Yes! But I want more. I grasp your collar and bring you up to me. You position yourself between my legs and enter me as we kiss deeply. My darling, my slave, my love, there is nothing like the feeling of you inside me! I scratch my nails down your sweating, heaving back in my ecstasy. You bend your neck and place your lips onto my breasts and bite my nipples. Reality inverts itself when I cum. How you love to hear me cum. The wetness floods around your penis and I smile that smile.

I move with you; it is your turn now. Cum for me, baby. You slide out of me and fall limp by my side, remembering to cover me with the sheet before falling in to a daze. I snuggle up next to you but only briefly as I might reignite too soon. I remove my toys from you and put on my robe. Rest up, darling.

you lie deliciously,
even as you pull away
from sharing yourself

There's a naked woman in your bed. I am sitting upright as you come and kneel behind me. You are to kiss and caress me until my skin burns hot to your touch, I become wet, my breath catches in my throat, and I flush pink. Can you contain yourself? I turn to nuzzle in your fur, loving your scent and the feel of your body against mine. Come to me, baby. Falling back, my juices all over your sheets as you slide inside. Fucking you is one long, exquisite orgasm as the head of your penis rubs over my G-spot. You feel so very, very good. In this light, your sweat makes your body glow. I wrap my legs around you and add my own motion to yours. More, more, more; hurry; YES! My muscles contract and twist around your penis and my juices burst forth. Oh my god! YES! More, more, more!

The preceding scenarios should give you a clear idea of what being a "soft dome" is about. Most men will find participating in such activities enjoyable and will readily volunteer. All you have to do is to give yourself permission to explore and enjoy their submission. To prove the point, one of my hopeful male sluts has added his voice to one of the preceding scenarios. You can now see this from his point of view. His words are italicized.

You take my leash in your hand and slowly begin to lead my wanting body into a private room so that you may have your way with me. This is what I have been longing for all evening, my time alone with my Mistress. My heart leaps in anxious anticipation of what you have in store for your willing slut. As we enter the room and you close the door behind us I notice the new toys you have laid out on the bed. I know tonight will be a completely explosive sexual experience! The sight of your naked body excites me; all of that lovely fur for me to nuzzle. The idea of all of that strength and power at my command is so delicious to me. I can sense that my Mistress is pleased by the sight of my naked body, and the pleasure begins to set in already, just the thought of pleasing you drives me crazy. I put my arms around you and kiss the side of your neck, breathe in your scent, delicious, and purr in your ear. You like my warm breath against your neck, don't you, darling. *"Always my love!" I reply.* Your eyes close and your legs part as I reach down to very slowly slide the vibrating probe up your ass. Feels good, doesn't it, sweet-heart. *Oh god, yes, is does Mistress... The vibrations make my balls feel so good as I feel the vibe slowly enter my ass.* I caress your penis, feeling it hardening beneath my touch. But no, you cannot cum just yet. *Yes, I know I am not permitted to cum yet; I clench my muscles and force myself to not reach orgasm just yet.* Your hand stroking my penis makes holding back difficult, but I manage to control myself knowing what may *lie in store for me if I am a well behaved slut. My mind shifts to other thoughts. I want desperately to feel your soft lips wrap around my penis, teasing it with your tongue. You stand there as I kneel down to suck your penis just enough to get the vibrating cock ring around it; easing it around your thicknesses. You have such a pretty penis.*

I sit and relax watching you feel the vibrations from my toys. *I bask ever so briefly at the site of your naked body sitting before me on the side of the bed, anticipating what we are to do next, what you will order me to do, and what I will do for my Mistress to ensure she is pleased this evening.* Then you kneel before me as I spread my legs for you. With my hands in your hair, you bend to lick and pay homage to me. *I enjoy kneeling before you, anxious with anticipation of tasting you when my mouth meets your vagina as it has so many times before. My penis throbs as I ravage you enjoying every minute of it. I feel your hands pushing my head closer and closer to you, my tongue going deeper and deeper inside of you as you tease me with the cock ring you so graciously allowed me to wear for the time being.* "Such a sweet slut," I whisper to you as you kneel there, your tongue very busy on my clit. *My penis throbs harder and harder as I suck on your clit; I want so badly to cum!* Oh yes, you are so very good with your mouth. I love the way the back of your shoulders look when you are kneeling before me; very tasty with all of those muscles. *I ask permission to run my hands over your back and ass as I lick you intensely. You grant me that indulgence.* I run my hands slowly over those shoulders enjoying the feel of your skin. *I run my hands over your smooth skin as I caress your clit with my tongue.*

I press the controls and send pulses to the vibrating cock ring. Your quivering responses are very seductive. "Mmmmmm, you are very, very good." *I manage to whimper: "Thank you, Mistress," as my penis throbs harder and harder.* You eagerly drink up my very wet orgasm. Your muffled groans of pleasure arouse me even more. Rolling orgasms run through me and the heavens turn inside out. *Yes! I begin to convulse as I feel your orgasm shower my mouth with your wet-ness. God, I want to penetrate you!* But I want more. I grasp your collar and bring you up to me. *Still being an obedient slave to my Mistress I take you in my arms and we fall together onto the bed, my face still slightly covered in your wetness. You moan as we collapse together, arm in arm in the heat of passion, both ready to please the other. My heart races as I feel your vagina gently slide around me as I slide my penis ever so slowly inside of you.* My darling, my slave, my love, there is nothing like the feeling of you inside me! I scratch my nails down your sweating, heaving back in my ecstasy. *I pull you tightly towards me to ensure you can feel the fullness of my erect penis.* You bend your neck and place your lips onto my breasts and bite my nipples. *I hear you let out a slight moan as I bite your left nipple.* Reality inverts itself when I cum. How you love to hear me cum. The wetness floods around your penis and I smile that smile. *I feel your vagina tense around me…. You are about to climax again.*

I move with you; it is your turn now. Cum for me, baby. *I can no longer hold myself, and I let myself go. I cum inside of you so hard you begin to moan and then an ever so subtle scream emerges from your lips. My Mistress is enjoying herself, I can tell. I feel your fingernails scratching me harder and harder as you let out gasps and screams. I thrust harder than before as my first orgasm passes. You let out one final loud scream as I finish cumming inside of you…* You slide out of me and fall limp by my side remembering to cover me with the sheet before falling in to a daze. *Your slave must take care of his Mistress after the pleasure she has granted him.* I snuggle up next to you, but only briefly as I might reignite too soon. The touch of your skin against mine has always excited me.

I remove my toys from you and put on my robe. Rest up, darling. *I take a deep breath and ponder what could possibly await me after the intense pleasure I just experienced.*

After such an experience, most men will be more than willing to return to you. But there will be those who will opt out. You must prepare yourself for rejection. Some men simply cannot get their minds around the concept of service.

midnight conversations
remembering touches
there in the darkness

In the dark, I stand next to you at first and then put my arm around you and breathe on your neck murmuring something to your earlobe. Close your eyes and imagine what sex with me would be like. My hand in your hair forces you to tilt your head back, and I kiss your throat before lightly teasing your lips with the tip of my tongue— perhaps I will kiss you—very, very lightly and fleetingly. A kiss from a wraith. Claws run slowly and lightly down your spine. Love biting the nape of your neck. Nothing about you is sacred. I will enjoy every inch of your body but so slowly, ever so slowly. Savoring. There in the dark.

In the dark, I crouch above your prostrate naked body feeling your warmth. Feeling the texture of your skin beneath my cheek as I caress you with my lips, the top of my knee resting snuggly up against your testicles. Lick a spot and then breathe on it. How would it feel getting this close to me? Claws run slowly and lightly up along the side of your hip. There is no escape for you now. There is no rest for you now. Each orgasm you have will only make you more vulnerable for the next. You have no limits with me. My skin sliding along your skin and fur. My hands, lips, and body reveling in yours. Hard, soft, pleasure, pain it's all there; in the dark.

In the dark, I seek your total disintegration to orgasmic sensory overload. I want you to quiver in both fear and delight. Once. To lose all vestige of control from anticipation alone. Cum for me; then cum again, and again, and again. Feel me alongside of you. Twice. Feel me around you. Slow, relentless, rhythmic. Timed to the beating of your heart. Will you resist? Can you resist? My lips on yours. My juices all over you. The long slow sliding into oblivion. Thrice. Sucking your fingers, you nipples, your penis. Feeding from you. Hair thin red lines sloping around your waist gently licked. Before I leave you, in the dark.

Men are relatively simple creatures with straightforward thought patterns. Wild, rampant, skin-on-skin, full-body-contact sex will usually weld them to your side, regardless of how you look, how you dress, or how much or little you weigh. When you are a domme, the more demanding you are the more in demand you are.

I have men come up to me in bars, kneel and kiss the ankle of my black leather, kitten-heeled boot, and all of the other men witnessing this wish whole-heartedly that it was them who were so privileged. Sneer at the hunger you see in their eyes, and you will only enhance your allure. But since we are being beguiling dommes, we do this with a sense of fun and lightness. Be ready to laugh with them over the irony of a big, strong alpha-male submitting to a pretty, little, fluffy kitten and you will win them. It is just in their nature, you see. But it is a huge ego boost for any woman, and it can change their lives for the better.

Let me make one issue very clear if I have not already done so. I do not condone, tolerate, or in any way promote domestic violence of any kind. You must trust, care both about and for, and respect your men for who they are. It takes a very strong and confident man to submit. Never raise your hand, empty or not, to him in anger.

The benefits of becoming a male slut are immediately apparent. The male gets more sex than he ever dreamed of receiving. Being selected by a domme also gives him confidence in himself. By pleasing her, he learns how to please women, making him more skillful and desirable to other women. His desires being fulfilled make him happier than before. His stress level is lower. He gets a vacation from decision-making. He gets a break from responsibility for a time. When life or work gets to be too much, he can seek temporary relief in a more healthy way than by drinking or drugging himself into oblivion.

One of the less apparent benefits is that usually he begins to see women as individuals, each desirable in her own way. He is more tolerant and understanding and is even friendlier toward women. One male described it as having his eyes opened after having been blind for so many years. One reason for this is that after taken care of everyone else for some time, men would like to be cared for themselves.

A responsible domme does care for her males and takes good care of them. She is concerned for them and their well-being. Being cherished in this way is good for them. Yet, you do have to let them off the leash every so often. Soft dommes are not usually into the 24/7 slavery ideology. I'd rather have men who choose to submit upon occasion with a gleam in their eye and a witticism on their lips than those who are completely and perpetually lost in adoration.

Then you might also want some time off yourself. I usually, according to my men, exhibit my need for time off by "turning left without signaling", that is by doing something not previously arranged or scheduled.

I also advocate playing within existing relationships whenever possible. Breaking up marriages should not be a part of any domme's plan. Life is frequently messy enough. There is no need to add any more "drama" to it.

I would venture to say that it is almost impossible for a human to be completely happy or healthy if they are devoid of a meaningful sexual relationship. Further, evidence suggests that where sex is actively prohibited, as within certain religions, then the sexual urge, being so strong, tends to manifest in abusive ways that cause great harm to human society.[3]

This does not only apply to men. Women too must come to understand and accept their sexuality regardless of how that sexuality manifests itself. However, you must never forget that he is worthy of your respect.

The reason why lust is described as a deadly sin is that it sees another person as a means to the end of our pleasure- it fails to value the human person and simply sees the function they can perform for us.[4]

Love and cherish your man or men as he or they will love and cherish you. For more on this and other related topics, I recommend *The Ethical Slut* by Dossie Easton and Catherine A. Liszt. Although, in style, this book may be a bit sentimental and romantic, the ethics presented are sound. It is also true that what one desires in the bedroom is not what one may desire out of the bedroom.

You may not really want your fantasies made real. This is fine. Sometimes fantasies should remain fantasies. There are not only personal reasons for this but also familial professional reasons for discretion. Your private and public lives should remain separate. Your children do not really need to know either. What you disclose will affect others, and the consequences might be devastating. Only your partner/partners need to know anything. Even so, do not expect your life as a domme to be free and easy sailing off into the sunset.

"I didn't want to be an accessory in a man's life; lingering on the periphery." Each of us wants and needs to be of central importance to another person. We need to be

---

[3] Geoff Haselhurst, Karene Howie, (January 2005) Email. http://www.Spaceand Motion.com. Copyright 1997 – 2005: Released as Copyleft / GNU Free Documentation License (FDL).

[4] Peter Vardy, Quotations from The Puzzle of Sex, 1997, p127.

involved in their lives. We need to involve them in our own life. We seek to discover the exact nature of the relationship so we can bond with that other person. Yet no relationship remains static. We therefore continue exploring. Interpersonal communication is not always pleasant, and the insights are not always welcome.

> *"I want more," she said.*
> *"Do you deserve more?" he asked.*
> *"I guess not," she answered.*

The damage, once done, never heals and is never forgotten. The relationship changes from this point. The message is very clear, the lesson well learned. Never ask. Never tell. Keep your heart from mine. Having ventured there once, she will never return.

> *"You do not tell me," he complains.*

Of course not. Now, she will never tell, and never seek any closer relationship with you. She will linger on your horizons for a time, and then gently fade away as a love lost. He will never know why. The point being that if he had to ask if she deserved more—"deserved"?—then the answer (for him) was obviously no. More she was not going to get, and she must be content with what little he was willing to give her. Very well. In his complaint, he has his results.

All relationships require some degree of work, even those between a Mistress and her slave. Each of us trains the other how to behave.

Very early on in their relationship, she asked once for sex. She initiated sex. He was perhaps tired but he did his best and very good it might have been except for a few words spoken after-wards. "The job of sex," he sneered at her. The message was clear. His superior attitude told her all she needed to know. For initiating sex, asking for sex, she was a slut. The damage was irreversible. Never again would she hurtle herself joyfully into his arms. Never ask. The leaping of her heart with desire for him would be crushed inside and kept from him. Never tell.

"We never have sex anymore, and I miss it," he complains.

The results were inevitable. One cannot demand a certain standard of behavior for any number of years and expect things to return, now that he has come to realize what he has lost, to what they once were and might now be. We teach each other over time and we learn over time. The two paths do not necessarily coincide.

Further discussion revealed that he did realize what he had done. Not then, but now. If the situation were repeated now, he admits that he would cut his heart out before saying what he once had. She remains unwilling to risk it with him. She makes spontaneous overtures but only up to a point. A kiss, a hug, a cuddle, but nothing more. Still she says nothing. Never ask. Never tell.

Sometimes the education is unintentional, as illustrated above. As a domme, you must be very careful when you are playing to not send the wrong message. This is why prior thought, discussion, and planning must be done.

I wish you well and hope that life treats you gently. Enjoy your new role! May it only bring you and yours happiness.

Biographic Note

The authoress is the most beguiling of dommes. She is married, and has been married to the same man for 28 years and counting, in spite of having had two rambunctious children, a postgraduate degree, and several careers.

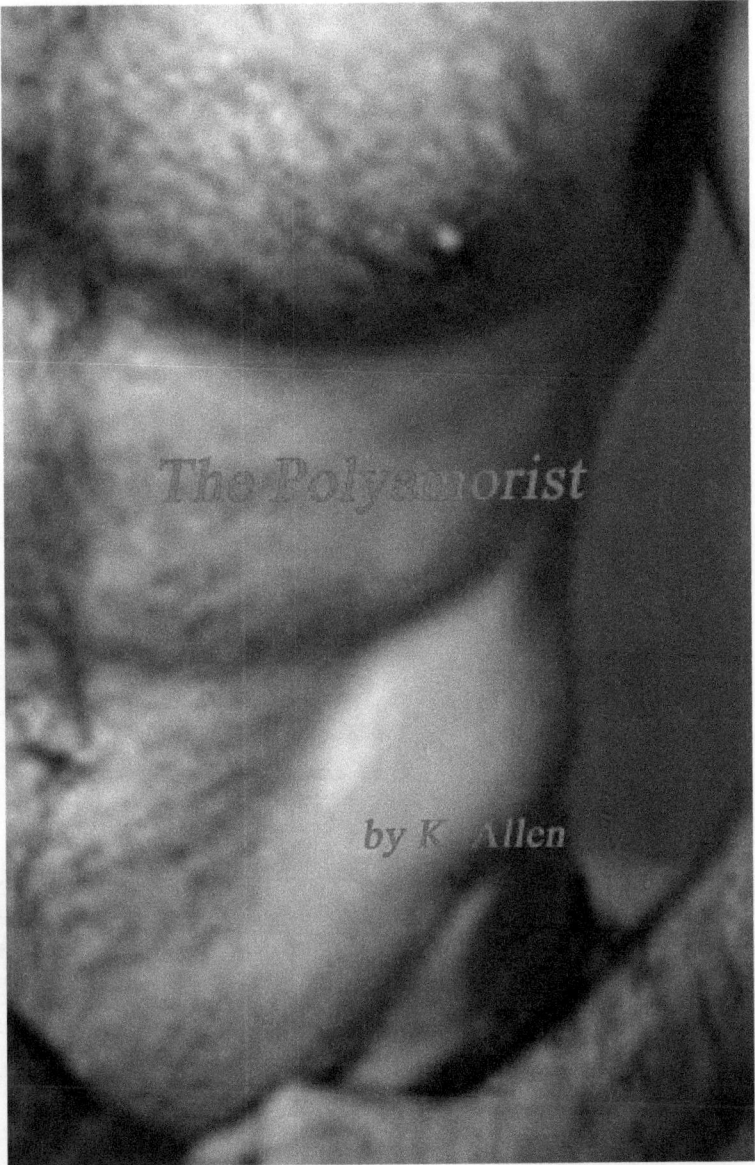

The Polyamorist

by K. Allen

by Corbis

dedicated to
Camden C. Cochran
with
an inordinate
amount of
affection

Polyamory is the non-possessive, honest, responsible and ethical philosophy and practice of loving multiple people simultaneously. Polyamory emphasizes consciously choosing how many partners one wishes to be involved with rather than accepting social norms, which dictate loving only one person at a time. Polyamory is an umbrella term, which integrates traditional multi-partner relationship terms with more recent terms. Polyamory is from the root words Poly meaning many and Amor meaning Love hence "Many Loves" or Polyamory.

http://www.polyamorysociety.org

Introduction

We have all been kicked in the teeth, one way or another, by someone we believed loved us. It happens. Life is not always the ideal dreamy wonderland of the fairytales where 'happily ever after' occurs. This is not to say that it cannot; simply that for some of us 'happily ever after' will be difficult to attain.

In some cases, the difficulty comes from having more than one choice. Sociologists, such as Desmond Morris, tell that we are happiest within our 'pair-bonds' which is defined as a reproductive pair: one male and one female. This may be true but it also maybe due to the lack of the truly polyamorous included in the study.

Polyamory is simply the ability to love more than one other person in an intimate relationship. That this can be achieved with some affection is beyond doubt given the historical evidence. But many believe that 'true love' can only be achieved once and then only with that one person. One falls in love, gets married, has children, and then one continues on living 'happily ever after'. That may well be the plan that society has in mind but it does not always work.

Polyamory can be two couples in an intimate interlocking relationship or in a couple with additional friends of both partners. It can also be 'swinging' where the couple actively seeks and maintains various intimate relationships with a circle of likeminded couples. There is to be no quibbling over terms.

How ever you wish to define polyamory, the important point is the relationship formed between the persons involved. Central to any intimate relationship is women's interaction with men. Your relationships with men have not been going well, have they? There is a way to fix this. We will begin the reclamation process by facing up. It may not be him. Admittedly, men have their flaws and issues but that is another book. It may be you. Confess that you may have committed errors and permitted your flaws to obscure your virtues—your 'best self'.

Some of the errors women make include playing games with men, competing with other women for men, chasing after unattainable men, accepting unworthy or incompatible men for the sake of having a relationship—any relationship, not reciprocating sexually and not openly, and honestly communicating with men. Do not make the excuse, "I'm just being me.' That hasn't worked. Be your best self instead.

Sincerity in your relationships is the key to sustaining them whether with one man or six men. Do not say it, unless you mean it, whole-heartedly and without reservation. Love as you should live – unstintingly.

Living whole-heartedly within a wider circle of intimate simultaneous relationships with various men is the subject of this book.

1.

"Men!" How often have women said that? I sometimes wonder how men get through the day with their faults being what they are. But then, I have faults of my own. So I say "Men!" with a wide grin and a hint of mischief. We are all a mix of the good, the bad, and the indifferent. Men are just the same. They are not some separate species. They are people similar to us. They have their joys, needs, desires, hopes, and sorrows just as we do. They are not ravening beasts bent upon your destruction. They are people worthy of your respect and affection.

Men do have their own methods and viewpoints. There is nothing inherently wrong or bad about this; this is just how it is. A man's difference is what makes him interesting.

Men often ask 'what do women want'. I do not know about women in general, and neither do you, but we both know, or should know, what we as individual women want. Think for a moment. What do you want in a man? What do you want from a man? There are many men out there so be sure of your target. This 'targeting' is also useful when it comes to selecting your hunting ground and then in selecting the one or two you want from the group.

Each man is different from all other men. Just as you are an individual, so are they. Whatever the last man did has nothing to do with this man here. Your ex was not reincarnated in the man before you. Let go of whatever baggage you have with you. He was not responsible for and should not be made to pay for what your ex did, or did not, do. Not only that, this man here, does not want to hear all about your ex either. Focus upon the real life before you. Focus upon the here and now. Upon this moment hangs this relationship.

Silencing the internal monologue can be difficult but if you are ever going to sustain a relationship, you will have to learn how to do it. Think for a moment if this man has given you any reason to fear or mistrust him. If he has then you leave. Life is too short as it is. Living with an unsatisfactory man is not necessary. But if he has not, then tell your inner voice to shut up and go away. Give him his chance. Listen to him. Look at him. See him. Focus upon him, as he is right here and right now. Do not worry about next week, next month, and next year. Stop worrying altogether. Enjoy a flirtation with him. If he wants more, he will let you know. If you want more, invite his participation. Give him your number and move along.

Men respect women who respect themselves. Visual clues include standing up straight, being socially poised and smiling, easily and comfortably saying hello and conversing with strangers. Verbal clues include being able to speak of various topics and not just those of interest to you, being able to flirt lightly, being ready to laugh and enjoy the wit of others. Can you say no? Can you say yes? Are you in control of yourself? If you know who you are, and what you want, you will appear confident and full of self-respect.

Trying your hand at hosting involves paying attention to details. For example, when introducing people do not stop at his or her name; mention something they can use to begin a conversation. "Maggie, this is James Conroy. Please find out about his new book for me." "Jim, this is Margaret Fitzwilliam and she's had so much trouble with her Corvette." Now if Jim is at all good with cars, they should get on very well.

How well do you take rejection? Men deal with this all of the time. If you can accept being told no, you will earn his respect. If he is not interested in you, do not chase after him. Politely standing up for yourself and your choices also earns respect. You can deal with the occasional 'what have I done?' later in private. Yes, we all have made mistakes but there is no need to drag them out into your conversations. Just as you should not 'future-think' so too should you not 'past-think'. What has been done has been done. Let it go.

Men are similar to women but they do deal with life in different ways than women do. Men do not spend a lot of time analyzing personal things to death. They use language differently. They do not employ sub-texts and meta-messages like women use them. Men also play by different rules; for example, they compete with other men for a place in the social and professional hierarchy earning and losing respect in the eyes of the other men. Women should never compete other than professionally. Anthropologists like to tell women that we compete with other women for the best genes. Perhaps we do, but we should not. We can learn to share.

Being one of the boys does not work. You are not male. You do not know the tribal rules. Your strength lies in being the one he looks for when he enters a social gathering and being the one he can quietly get drunk with sitting and laughing on the porch in the summer twilight. You are the one he can love and intimately enjoy. Being your best self without pretence is what you need to do.

Exercise #1. Finding you best self.

List your flaws – be honest. Then list what you have to do to correct them and then do it. Monitor your progress. For example, I tend to interrupt people. I am aware that this is characteristic of feminine speech patterns but that does not make it any more acceptable. I now make a conscious effort not to interrupt. And I will ask my 'date' how I did after social interactions as a way of monitoring my behavior.

Exercise #2. To increase your social poise and conversational skills.

At a social gathering, calmly mingle and make it a point to meet and speak intelligently with everyone there about that person's topic of interest. Be sure to ask three questions about his topic and listen to his answers. If they ask you for your opinion, tell them you have not yet formed one. Above all, do not argue. This is not a debating society.

When you get home and are alone, write down names, topics discussed and everything you can remember about that person into a small notebook. Stick to facts. Do not write in that so and so was a jerk. Only facts are of any interest, no gossip, and no opinions.

Exercise #3. To increase your self-awareness

Record your conversations using a small micro-recorder, only your voice is needed here so keep the mike on you alone. Forget you are wearing it. Afterwards, replay the tape and see if you like that women. Do you constantly repeat yourself? Are you returning to the same old themes? Do you sound desperate, tired, or bitter? Do you talk only about yourself? Are you depressing or desperate? If you answered yes to any of the above, you are killing your relationships before they have even begun. Think before you speak. Listen to what you are saying. Joy and vivacity attract people to you.

Exercise #4. To discover how others perceive you

When you talk to a man, do you lightly touch him? Try it. Moving through a crowd, say excuse me while lightly touching him. When laughing at a joke, lightly touch the man who is next to you who is also laughing. Men will not bite. You do not need to fear light social physical contact with them. Note if they shy away or if they smile at you.

These exercises are meant to increase your social poise and confidence in general as well as to decrease your mistrust and fear of men in particular. By practicing them, you will also learn to converse with people, not at them, and will improve your memory for faces and names. You may also learn interesting things on various topics that you can later use in your conversations. By being focused outwardly towards other people, you will make yourself more aware of others and your impact upon them.

Exercise #5 To practice giving (reciprocating), try the next exercise.

Before going out, develop in your mind a general plan for the evening. What do you want to achieve and how will you go about helping that to happen? Think it through systematically. You are not going to be able to follow your plan exactly but you should be actively engaging others. Participate. Give a little. Venture a small joke. Flirt a little bit. Ask someone to dance perhaps. Try to keep moving towards this evening's goal but keep it light and airy—it may not happen tonight. No harm done, just move along and try again later or elsewhere. See how many phone numbers or kisses you can collect, for example. Laugh and make a sort of game of it.

2.

Younger women have their own set of problems. Almost every man on the planet actively pursues them and they are not quite sure of what is what yet. Younger women rarely know themselves. They are not sure of what they want. It is like living in a whirlwind. School, career, men, expectations, all of it is wildly out of control and she feels very vulnerable.

Nevertheless, you the younger woman, can still present the proper image of being an independent woman worthy of a man's regard while having fun. Take a deep breath and prepare to go swimming with the 'big girls'!

The first thing you have to do is to calm down and tone it down. Yes, we know, sweetheart, but you really are not winning friends and influencing the right people by getting drunk or doped up out in the parking lot while giving some guy you just met a blowjob in his car. Forgive my bluntness.

Relationships with men are not just about sex. There is some intimacy involved as well. The more you interact with men, the better you understand them. This may not translate into liking them or loving them as a gender on the whole, but it does make it easier to deal with them individually. It is true that if all conversational gambits fail, there is little you can do other than unbuttoning his shirt. At least try to get his name before it comes to that.

Younger women have the reputation of being slightly scatterbrained, silly, and shallow. This is not the sort of reputation you will need or should desire. Being lively does not require you to be silly.

What you have to do is to focus upon the person, not on the packaging. Learn to make intelligent choices in your playmates. Does he do what he says he will? Does he do what he said he wouldn't? If a man does not show you respect, you quietly drop him off your roster. If a man becomes violent, you have him arrested; no debate. You are only here for fun.

The point is to have the widest social circle as is possible. Learn how to interact with all kinds of people in a positive way. Do not try to manipulate people and do not play the diva. Conversely, do not be all shy and timid either. Just be your best self.

A.

Young men, in particular, are unsure of themselves just as you are. Help both of you out by being clear and undramatic. Do not ask for Sir Galahad on his white horse. Do not let flattery go to your head. You are not 13 anymore either. There are consequences for your actions now that you are an adult.

Make absolutely sure of your health status. Practice safe sex religiously. If he does not wear a condom, there will be no sex, period. There is no discussion on this topic and no compromises. Yes, we know all about sensation, but it is not worth dying for. You are responsible for birth control. Take care of it.

PMS is not an acceptable excuse for your poor behavior. You are accountable for your actions, speech, and behavior. Being drunk or high is also not an acceptable excuse for being nasty or a total bitch. Men will take it once, but not twice. Women will not take it at all. The idea here is to gain friends not enemies. You want the widest social circle possible, since this will help you in the future.

Do not compete for men. You have no reason to compete. No one else is exactly like you. Cooperate and be a good girlfriend when it is your turn. Do not put potential dates through an inquisition. It is not necessary. He will show his true character in time. Remember to keep it light and play the field. There are enough men out there, so you all can share and share alike.

School and career come first. You fit men in when and where you can. Young men are in the same position as you are so do not expect gifts and fancy dinners. If he chooses to spend his money on flashy cars and so forth, fine. It is his money. If he chooses to play the field, fine, it is his prerogative as a single male. Fair is fair.

Limit your competitiveness to your profession. Relationships are only for fun. This is especially true of relationships with young men. If he is not fun, you say goodbye.

Young women also must have a do not ask, do not tell policy. Learn to be discreet. Your personal life is your business and only your business. No one else has a need to know. You never ask nor do you ever answer prying personal questions. You never hear let alone spread malicious gossip. Be kind and civil to everyone you meet.

That being said, I must point out that for some men you are prey. For safety reasons alone, always leave a note of where and with whom you will be and when you expect to return with a roommate or a friend. Carry a working cell phone at all times set on vibrate. If you live alone, get a dog—a large dog. Be prepared to be responsible for your own transportation.

When meeting a man alone for the first time, do so in a public place with lots of people there and have a safety call made to you about 15 minutes into the conversation. Do not make a big deal about it—keep it cool. You are just checking in.

If you agreed to a date, keep it. Only disease and your death excuses you from a date once made. There is no such thing as getting a better offer. Keep a day planner and use it. Your social life should be as orderly as it possibly can be even if work interferes sometimes. If you break a date, you must do so well in advance and suggest an alternative date. You always offer to split the costs.

Young men are less mature than women of the same age. Relax and do not demand perfection from him. You expect him to be polite, and fun; nothing more.

Sexually he may also not know very much or have a great deal of skill so do not expect it. Sex is best when there is some affection with it but it is also rather good without it. Learning what each other likes, dislikes, and would like to try can be fun. Be open to exploration but keep your head. It is not love; it is lust. Buying you a single red rose because he got his hair cut is love. Wanting to share a bed with you is lust.

If you do not care for his style and he refuses to learn, be prepared to say no and mean it. If he is rude about it, ignore him. Once you have made your decision, do not go back on it. Do not tease him sexually unless you mean to go through with it. Do not say one thing and do another. You will only confuse and spoil him for others. You do not want the next girl to pay the price. If you do not want him, just say 'no thank you' and move on. Remember the rule: no games.

Marriage and then children are best done when in your twenties. This is just a fact. Your personality can deal with change and your body can deal with childbirth best when you are in your twenties. The man with the courage to ask you to marry him is usually the one you want. Yet, do not be in a tremendous rush to wed. The qualities needed in a husband, and a father, are not the same as those you want in a boyfriend; similar but not identical. Wait for him to declare himself. You do have some time.

B.

While you are waiting, consider the other men available to you. Thus far, we have been speaking of young men; those society thinks you should marry. But there are advantages to older men. They have a great deal of social and sexual skill. They are also full-grown men with careers, resources, and history behind them. Older men have a track record. Exploring that track record may be an adventure you might not want to miss.

Men above the age of 35 are usually married, divorced, separated, or never married. You will want to avoid those who have never married. If he is also a virgin, you should run away as fast as you can. The 40-year-old male virgin is not a joke. If no one found him acceptable, there is usually a good reason why they have not, and you do not need to find out those reasons firsthand.

Married older men are play toys, pure and simple. Have fun but do not expect anything to come of it. You have to accept that you will see him when he can and not necessarily when you would like to see him. His situation at home is his business. Be civil asking about his family but do not pry. Do not ask for more than he can give you. Accept that you will always come second in his life to his wife and his children.

Separated and divorced men over 35 are fair game. Have fun with them while remaining open to possibility of more to come. With these men, their motives for playing out of their age group matter. Ask them. If they are bitter about their ex-spouse, take it with a grain of salt. The faults probably were not all hers. Clear the baggage out of the way and then expect him to leave it behind him.

He may want to have children. You have to consider this possibility. In this case, marriage will be offered. You will then have to balance his expectations with yours. Does he swing, for example? Are there children from previous marriages? Remember his history and how do you feel about that? Can you deal with being thought his daughter and not his wife?

Please note, even his family will corner you to question your motives and test the strength of your bond with him. Since society thinks you are dating where you shouldn't, there will be hard times.

"And because religious and secular law were for centuries so closely intertwined, the 'morality of sex'—a purposeful myth that has been productive of more guilt and misery than any other aspect of human or divine law- has remained an important factor in social control."[5]

It is amazing how pervasive this idea of social control is. Even his children will question and fight you. Are his kids are older than you are? Are his grandkids older than you are? There is a family hierarchy and they may feel you are over-stepping your boundaries. Can you trade in the exuberance of young men for the more arcane pleasures of older men? Date him and enjoy him, sure; learn from him; but marriage and children is a huge deal. If you decline the honor, he will leave you. Just as when your young Mr. Right comes and asks you to marry him, you will leave the older man.

Independent women of any age are the most desirable. The independence matters, not just the youth. Bimbos may be fun for a while but their attraction palls quickly. Having brains, beauty, and the ability to cook—and seeing the rueful humor in that cliché—is what counts. You should look for the same independence in your men.

Dealing with multiple men can be simple. Refuse to discuss the one with the other. Male tantrums and possessiveness is never tolerated. Jealousy is the mark of a man with low self-esteem. Do not play into his game by apologizing to him. You are not doing anything wrong, he is. Do not agree to meet him to say goodbye. Just cut him out of your life. Should you remain in the same circles just be civil, polite, and completely indifferent to him while keeping your distance.

---

[5] Tannahill

Exercise #1. To develop independence

Go to a movie you want to see by yourself. Then go to an art gallery or museum by yourself. It is not as much fun as going with friends but it does help develop a more independent mindset. It will also give you more topics for conversation.

Exercise #2. To show your independence

Pick up tickets to something he might like and invite him out. In this case, you are paying the freight. Are you comfortable with this? If money is tight, take him on a picnic or something similarly priced and make no apologies.

Exercise #3. Useful for those dating an older man

Take him to the zoo and watch the people around you. See how they react to you two as a couple. Can you handle it? This is a kind of self test. Also, by taking the initiative, you begin to develop your independence and your ability to make decisions for more than just yourself.

C.

There is nothing wrong with looking before you leap, but shyness—the inability to have fun once you have leapt—is not something you need. Stop it. Once you have made a decision, act upon it. If you find you have made a mistake, as we all have, you extricate yourself with a becoming grace and do not repeat it. Once should be enough. Twice is just being silly.

Manage your money wisely, work at your career, play all of the field being careful to play fair and all will be well.

Go forth and enjoy!

3.

Older women have baggage; but then, so does anyone who has lived for awhile. You may have children, other obligations or problems, and work. Your time is not always your own. This is especially true if you are married and you want to stay married. Sustaining a relationship takes care, consideration, attention, and some work. Yes, I know how life can get in the way, but you have to try. See if you cannot fit time with him in somewhere. Regardless of how polyamorous you, and he, might be, continuing in your primary relationship is very important. If you need help, get it from professionals not your friends.

Spending quality time with your husband is important even if you are not doing anything in particular. Do not stop having sex with him. No matter what shape the two of you are in, there is always some thing that can be done by each of you for each of you. Exploring your options can be fun too. So your sex drives aren't what they used to be. Cuddle up, begin nuzzling, and see what happens.

A.

Generally, men do not care if you are married if the likelihood of them remaining alive is good. Men do not like drama anymore than you do. Messy emotional scenes are to be avoided if at all possible. Deal with the problem, if it is a problem, in an adult manner. This works both ways. Do not create a scene if, for example, you find out he has been having affairs. It is much more effective to explore why he has been having affairs than to get into fights in the divorce courts. It may be him. It may be you. Either way, open and honest if tactful communication is the important thing. It may be difficult, but behave in an adult fashion and stay calm. If it is you who is having the affairs, you have to clearly understand and be able to articulate your motives if called upon to do so. Deal with any feelings of guilt on your own. Playing in the big leagues demands that you be a big girl. Tearful midnight confessions are just not on. Discretion begins by keeping your own counsel. No talking out of school.

Do you have to divorce him? Does he have to divorce you? The answer is no unless someone's safety is in jeopardy. If divorce is the choice, then get your lawyer and your financial advisor together with his and work out an equitable arrangement that leaves neither party impoverished. We are adults and these things happen even in the best of families. There is no need for anyone to take sides here. The only requirement is that you both whole-heartedly agree upon a specific course of action and develop a specific kind of relationship.

Instead of divorcing him, you could accept his being polyamorous. You too could be poly-amorous if you wished. You can love more than one man at a time. He can love more than one woman at a time. There is little wrong with having a wide social circle with a few special friends with whom you enjoy silken dalliance if you both agree to it. You may be surprised, but once all is out in the open and an agreement on ground rules has been reached, you will feel better than before. You can relax and enjoy life. Now it is a matter of scheduling. What about your children? If you do not play at home, there should be no problem. Get a reliable sitter if needed. Older children should be able to deal with the concept of guests in your home. There is no need to explain that he slept in your bed. More than most likely, they do not want to know. You only bring home those friends with whom you have a firm relationship in any case. Try for a 'friends with benefits' arrangement where there is mutual liking and respect as well as sex. Sex is better when there is affection and laughter with it. Polyamory is possible and enjoyable. Live and love unstintingly.

B.

Too late, you say? You are now divorced, angry, and bitter. Sorry, honey, but you will have to get over it. Let it go or resign yourself to a loveless life. You are now back to stage one. Time now to regain your independence and begin living the life you really want to live. Stop complaining about problems, your ex, and your difficulties—get on with fixing them. Then let them go.

Your dating pool is smaller now. Most men, of your age, are chasing young women, or they are married themselves. Nevertheless, there are men who will be seriously interested in you. Some of them will be younger than you are. How do you feel about that? For some men, you will be the 'younger woman'. How do you feel about this? What qualities in a man do you want? Just as you planned how you wanted an evening to go in one of the previous exercises, try to develop an idea of how you want the rest of your life to go. To borrow a dictum from foxhunting, "Plan your hunt, hunt your plan." What is your plan?

C.

Young men usually go through a stage where an older woman is the most attractive woman on earth. You become his Cleopatra. It is that hint of the forbidden that drives them. He becomes your boy toy. You get ardent sex and he gets his education. It is a fair trade if you can stand the heat. You will get the same sort of disapproval that a young woman dating an older man gets.

Younger men tend more toward drama and exuberance more than towards subtlety and skill. They are often reckless and unthinking. Can you deal with his being heedless of the consequences? Can you keep up socially and culturally? Sexually you win hands down. It is all of the other little things that make a younger man difficult to live with. He also has his career to think about. These are turbulent times for him and his behavior will often times reflect this.

Society is concerned with people being taken advantage of and getting hurt. If you play fairly there is no need for you to apologize. Just be prepared to face the trials ahead. Be careful to maintain equality in the relationship. This can be difficult especially if he is the same age as your children. You are not his mother and even young men will balk at being a 'leash-puppy' eventually. These relationships are usually short term if it's a primary relationship.

D.

Regaining your independence means burning your baggage in the back yard, figuratively speaking of course. What you want now is sincerity and affection in your relationships. You want them stable and long term. This may mean playing with men who have also been through the mill of divorce. Dealing with his bitterness and disappointment takes sympathy and stamina. It also takes a thick skin. He may want someone in her twenties too. This is not you. If he is not ready for you, you may have to move on. If he is after a 20-year old to bear his children, you may have to step aside. You should be prepared to do this with grace.

Is it worth it? Yes it is. Wisdom is bittersweet. I go into every relationship knowing, full well, that at some point, 'this is going to hurt'. I do it anyway. Good relationships enhance life and are worth every effort and every bit of pain. Wise women do not have bad relationships since they do not go with the wrong men. Men will also practice selection. If you do not see him again, he is not interested. Let him go. Move on. There are more men out there. There is no need to chase after disinterested men. There is no need to compete with the 20-year-olds either. You will have your lovers; there is no need to despair or to rush. Just do not sit at home and do not be a depressing drag when you go out. Laughter attracts; so laugh and go have fun. Join something off beat or unexpected. Participate in life. Try saying 'yes, I would love to' at every possible opportunity. No chickening out either! If you say 'yes I will', then yes, you will.

As a single female, you will be in demand by couples in the swinging set. This may be new to you. It is a great way to meet people who are well, shall we say uninhibited. Most of the women will be bisexual. If this is your thing okay, if not, that is okay too. Just be prepared to meet with various proposals. There are always single men available as well. If it seems that I am advocating swinging, you are correct. I am advocating swinging. Much of what you have learned or been taught about sex, men, and relationships is wrong. This was done for a reason.

"By the beginning of recorded history, authoritarian societies had already discovered that by disciplining sexual relationships it was possible to exercise a control over the family that contributed usefully to the stability of the state."[6]

Swinging is a useful way of re-educating yourself. It also puts you in the way of meeting people who will not judge you unduly. Try doing the exercises in the first section with a swing group. These people are not monsters nor are they sick or weird. They are people who just believe differently and live differently than you do. Swinging is also a great deal of fun!

One thing about swinging takes some getting used to. This is that the women determine who will do what with whom. The women involved choose all the relationships. If the ladies do not agree, then nothing will happen. The men will chat with you but nothing more until given permission by their wives.

---

[6] Tannahill

If you find you cannot let go of your previous education, ask yourself what do you fear will happen? Your lifestyle will change over time as your needs and desires change. Once again, there is no need to rush into anything. Moreover, you can stop whenever you wish. Being open to new experiences is the goal. Try everything twice, just to make sure.

E.

One of the issues with older women is their perception of their bodies. Some of you may be overweight. Most of you are not, you just think you are unattractive to men. Men are not so parochial. Height-weight proportionate (HWP) is enough for most men. This means that you have a waist and are taller than you are wide.

We are not '20-something hardbodies' any more. Some of us never were. Nevermind. Forgive us our figure flaws as we forgive yours. Remember it is the person not the packaging that truly matters. Beauty may or may not last but being obnoxious usually does.

If you are not in shape, and want to be, then just do it. There is no need to make it headline news. My personal diet and exercise plan involves not eating and having wild rampant skin on skin full body contact sex as frequently as possible. It works too.

Please leave all health issues at home when you venture out unless it will directly impact your date. You do not want to give the impression that you spend every other week in the hospital. You also do not want to give him the idea that you will break if he hugs you.

As an older woman, you are expected to have some control over your life. This may be easier said than done and bad things do happen to good people, but whining about it is never acceptable. If you have a problem, fix it. Go to Plan B if necessary. This may take some courage but you have courage; you are reading this book. Martha

Stewart may not be your queen, but she took something she was good at and made it work for her. Why not you?

F.

Here are a few notes on various situations that you may find useful.

Threesomes and foursomes are fun and enjoyable. There are various configurations and I suggest you try them all at least once. Ask one of your swinging friends to set one up for you. Ask two of your lovers, whom you think will get along well, if they would care to indulge with you. What do you do not want are men who will 'high five' each other over your back. Always give as good as you get.

When you are playing with a couple or couples, remember that his first obligation is to his wife. You are delightful but still second. Perhaps the two of you can gang up on him and see how much he can take before he cries 'uncle'? There is no reason why the ladies cannot be sexually aggressive.

Group sex parties in various sizes are a lot of fun. You will have the opportunity to play with all the men there either singly or in pairs or whatever. No man is likely to say no in these situations. Remember to be social with the ladies whose men you are borrowing and enjoying. If you can bring a man along to share with them, they will appreciate it. The main thing is to participate.

Please practice safe sex. Condoms remain mandatory even if birth control is no longer required.

Final note: reciprocate when it comes to sex. This is about mutual pleasure and shared orgasms. If you do not thrill him after he has thrilled you, he will not return for more. Men enjoy many of the same things you do. There is no secret about it; caress him, hold him, kiss, lick, bite, scratch—whatever he likes—do it. If you like something, tell him about it. Most men are more than merely willing to give you whatever you desire. Usually they are extremely delighted to comply with whatever you would care to suggest. Also, be sure to tell him what you do not like. Being responsive and participating gives everyone great joy and better sex.

4.

Having a multiple male household may strike you as being a bit odd, at least at first. Having two or three men around all of the time may seem crowded but it can work out very well. You have the master bedroom suite and each of the men has his own bedroom and bathroom. All other areas for common areas owned and used by everyone. Dividing the household chores can be a bit of a balancing act.

What usually ends up happening is that the men sort themselves out into a kind of domestic hierarchy. They do this on their own and without consulting you. This is good. Stay out of it. How you arrange the household budget is up to you but I recommend getting it all down on signed papers that are legally binding but not totally unbreakable. Consult with your lawyer and your financial advisor before entering into any agreements of this kind.

Even with resident males on the premises, you may want to have one or two, or more, non-resident men to play with. This too can be done, so long as all are aware and agree to the lifestyle, all will be well. Sounds rather a queen with a male harem, doesn't it? The reverse situation can also be done; that is, a king with his harem of women. It is your choice in either case.

You could even have two entire households more or less joined together, where the kids run in and out through both houses. This would be full, as opposed to partial, polyamory.

Society will not accept any such arrangement of course, so discretion will have to be maintained. Just put the house number on the mailbox and have an unlisted phone number. Tell your children and relatives to get over it, if you tell them anything at all.

What do you do when the men want to bring in other women? Are you jealous? If they use their own bed and not yours, would that be acceptable? Will you be welcoming?

Will you also participate? You have to confront all of the issues before entering into such a household. This includes the man who wants to marry, have children, and bring his wife into the household. Can you share? Will you help raise their children?

A.

Do you work from home? Bringing your employment home with you can create the need for more room and additional discretion and security. Who pays which bills? What happens if you, the queen, let us say, dies? Where does that leave your men? Consult everyone involved and get it all worked out beforehand. Consult your lawyer.

To see if you might like to set up one of these households, invite two of your male friends, who get along well, to spend a long weekend with you simultaneously including sleeping over in your bed. Do this several times.

Then, invite both of them to come and live with you. At first, they are to retain their own households and pay their own bills. You remain solely responsible for your new augmented household and its bills. Should all go well for say a year or so, all three of you should decide if making the arrangement permanent is feasible and desirable. This is when you bring in the professionals.

One of the latest developments has been the application of business partnership law to poly-amorous relationships, the Relationship LLC.

Now There Is A New Way To Tie The Knot. It is our position that limited liability companies, "LLCs", may prove to be the new marriage model. Marriage is presently available only to one man and one woman. LLCs are available to everyone, couples (of any sexual mix) who wish to pursue life together, a single parent family and groups of friends. Marriage is based on family law, limited liability companies are based on partnership law and the legal arrangement its "members" agree to.

http://www.relationshipllc.com/

This could be a useful alternative to the com-mingled household as only the assets of the LLC itself would be involved if the partnership were to end.

B.

Usually what happens is a couple decides to 'swing' and joins a 'swing group'. They then decide to 'host', that is to open their home to their friends for a party or two. Over time, they develop the intimate interlocking relationships we have been exploring. But they do not join their households into one. There are 'swing communities' where people who share in this lifestyle can live close to each other. This makes it easier on all concerned and eliminates the need for a commingled household.

5.

I make it sound so very easy. It can be easy. But there are some problems you and the men involved will have to solve.

A.

Jealousy destroys relationships. Regardless of cause, you have to be able to share and share alike if you enter this lifestyle. You may lay down whatever ground rules you all can agree upon, but one that is done, and all are abiding by those rules –you have to be able to trust and let go. If you cannot do this, then this lifestyle is not for you.

Even if you do not swing or are just dating, jealousy will kill your relationship dead. Jealousy says that you fear what is out there, that you do not trust your man or men, and that you have low self-esteem, that you are not 'good enough' some how. Rid yourself of these thoughts and emotions by confronting them head on. What do you really fear? Why do you fear this?

Some people manipulate through weakness. This is the 'if you leave me I will kill myself' defense. They prey upon your goodness and guilt to keep you locked in their jealous embrace. Life is too short to have to deal with such people. Rid yourself of them by getting in touch with your 'best self' and standing up for yourself. Do not do this kind of manipulation either. Fair is fair. If you would not tolerate such behavior from him, do not give it to him either.

Some, men especially, rule through intimidation. They angrily say 'you make me do this' and then burn your clothes. Call the police. This is one man who should not be out walking the streets. If this is you, then you have to change. Such violence is not ardent love. Whether it is you or him, get help now.

Actually watching your lover with another can be enlightening. When he is with you, you are too involved to really notice all that much. I was not aware that nibbling his fingertips during coitus would excite him so until I witnessed this when he was with another lady. Interesting, the fact that he could satisfy two sexually aggressive women more or less simultaneously boosted his self-confidence enormously. This is not an easy thing for a man to do but he did it very well. That is to say, everyone learns from the experience.

B.

From the ground rules, to which bills are paid by whom, to who everyone is, and the scheduling; there is a lot to remember. The organization you practiced before will come in handy now. This life can get very confusing as you try to get everyone's schedules to mesh. If you think you are bus and that your life is hectic now, just wait. You have not seen anything yet! Adding in your work, his work, their work and then the kids' schedules can be enough to make your computer sign up for early retirement. Then add in the local swing club meetings and the various parties, business trips and vacations—did I mention the holidays?—and you can see how quickly your once orderly life can become total chaos. You could then add in his family coming to visit when yours wants to visit. If you want to clean the house, hire a service! Sign up for grocery delivery and pick-up dry cleaning service. This is heavy duty socializing and you will have to be prepared to face this.

C.

You will also have to face society's wrath. The best you can hope for is to be ignored if word of your life gets out. Think about the young kids in school being asked what Daddy does for a living. Most alternatively living people keep their private lives very private indeed. This is also why various self-segregated communities develop. This is another reason to have a wide social circle of friends who will, in general, support you. Certain states and their legislatures will make laws that hinder your life. So remaining socially aware and continuing being involved in your community is a wise practice. This is also why I recommend a 'no evidence' rule of no possibly compromising pictures, or videos permitted.

6.

With the best effort and will in the world, sometimes, things just do not work out. Circumstances and situations do change over time. Perhaps it is time to break up and go your separate ways.

If you had papers drawn up, then it is time to consult the lawyers. This is especially true if you formed a Relationship LLC since business law governs these agreements.

If you were just dating or in a relationship without any papers or agreements, you have two choices before you; to part as friends or to be just a memory without any further contact.

A.

If there is to be no further contact between you, then it makes life easier. All you have to do really is to say 'goodbye' and then leave them alone. This does not mean that you cannot part on good terms. Perhaps you had agreed that if he found someone else, you would not stand in his way. For example, if he wanted a wife and children but could not with you and the prospective wife did not care to share. You would graciously step aside in such a case and gently retreat from his life. Remember him fondly and move on. It will hurt but it is part of being alive.

B.

You enjoy each other but you simply cannot live together. Perhaps he has been transferred elsewhere by his employer, or you have. Situations change. Nevertheless, you can remain friends. Exchange information and chat frequently. Trade pictures back and forth. Keep each other informed and involved in your life by using all available means and media. You may even break down and write an actual letter! You do the exact opposite of fading out from his life. Actively continue the relationship. This is much easier now that we have the Internet. I encourage you to use it.

I myself have just 'spoken' via email with a friend of many years with whom I had fallen out of touch. It was like no time had passed at all! We were still friends and confidants after all of these years! I have three women friends and we are all living in various states exchanging mails, kid pictures, and grandbaby pictures—as well as chatting about our various loves, of course. And, I am having a lunch with an ex-lover but still friend next Wednesday.

7.

My dream or goal is to be a rich widow with a nice house in the far suburbs stocked with cold champagne and hot men. What is your goal? What steps are you taking, legally now—do not get carried away here—to make your dream a reality? I am saving up. Are you? If not, why aren't you?

Just as you formed a general plan for an evening in a previous exercise, so to should you now plan the rest of your life. Be specific when outlining the steps you will need to take to realize your goal. I, for example, have selected my house plans, and the two men with whom I would like to live.

Younger women may find this step more difficult to do simply because they have no real idea of where they want to end up. Nevertheless, I encourage them to try. Now your life may not go as you had planned, but having a plan that you are actively pursuing will make your choices more clearly defined. Does option A move you toward or away from your goal? Is option B a better choice? Only you can decide these points.

8.

You can use the Internet to help you find people and groups in your area. Just be careful to check the sites out carefully beforehand. Read everything twice to make sure you have all of the information.

Be careful what you put onto the web because you do not have any control over the information or who uses it. We all like to assume that the world is a wonderful place but there are dangerous people out there. Use a more cautious type of judgment than you normally would.

A.

When writing up your profile, you do not want to be dishonest since that will decrease its effectiveness, but generally the more precise your language, the less you can say and therefore, the less you give away. You can always go and tell more when you actually meet a person off-line. But once you have lied, you can never get that back.

Making up different personae and pretending to be what you aren't is not being effective. You do not want to spend your time on-line; you want to meet the right people off-line. Bear this in mind when writing. Keep your goal in sight.

Some of these sites are communities and you can find yourself being embroiled within them. You can get caught up in an alternative kind of on-line lifestyle with its fights, grudges, and gossip. Do not do it. Keep your goal in mind when on-line.

B.

Many of these sites allow you to post photographs. Others actively encourage you to post photographs. Be careful with this. You do not want to show your face nor do you want to show something explicitly sexual. Erotic is fine but your identity should not be immediately evident.

Also, do not be quick to move from email to instant messaging. Do not give out your home number; use your cell number instead. Have simple business-like cards made up with your name and cell number on them to hand out when meeting someone assuming you like him well enough to go on a second date with him.

When meeting for the first time, do so in a public place that is relatively busy. Morning coffee, after work drinks, and lunch are all good 'first dates'. If you are very unsure, have a friend call your cell during the date to 'check in' with you and see how you are doing. Good second dates involve dinner and/or going to some event, a play or a movie, etc. After that, it is up to you to decide where you want to go from here.

C.

Perhaps you would feel more comfortable joining a group. Many sites have small gatherings called 'meet and greets' to which anyone wishing to come are invited. These are usually held after work or after 9 pm on weekends in some local tavern or eatery. These are excellent 'mingling' impromptu parties. Cards are a good idea for these events, since it is hard to remember everyone.

D.

Your place or his place? I vote for his place. When and how this happens is up to you. Bringing him back to your place should come after you have seen his. Caution befits a woman who is out on her own.

There is one rule you must never violate. Never just show up. There must always be some conversation before you walk into his place or he into yours.

If you plan on entertaining, stock up on towels and have a couple of bathrobes available. Masculine toiletries would be nice.

If you are a swinging couple, have an extra bedroom and bathroom and stock them for your guests and paramours. Do not use the master suite, which is reserved for you two alone. This may seem silly, but humans often are silly. This is one example of doing something special for your primary relationship.

Now all you have to do is to attend to your scheduling!

9.

Men are allegedly simple creatures, but if this were actually true, relationships would be much easier than they are. You have to begin understanding and treating them as people similar to yourself.

Finding your 'best self' and always presenting this to the men you meet is important. As it wears upon your, this only showing your virtues, you will gradually show you flaws, giving him time to get used to them. But then, by only being your 'best self', you may find yourself actually becoming your 'best self' as you conquer your flaws.

Now, go get them, sweetheart!

Example of Polyamorous Relationship Agreement

RELATIONSHIP AGREEMENT

The following persons, (XXXX) and (YYYY) freely enter into this relationship agreement, which will begin _____ 20__, extend for a period of one year, and terminate on _____, 20__. We are defining our relationship as a(n): (Open Dyad). At the expiration of this agreement, we may choose to reconfirm or renegotiate our agreement. Or we may choose not to continue our relationship and to part from each other peacefully, respectfully, and as whole and free persons.

(Name)(Name) Dated: _____, 20___

I freely enter into this contract, choosing to live in the NOW with you and remaining open-hearted to future expansion of our family. We know nothing is guaranteed and "happily ever after" exists only in fairy tales. Love and relationships take conscious, consistent effort to maintain and to flourish.

I am free to make commitments and I accept responsibility for my actions. My freedom comes from the personal expression of my own power. No one can take away my power to be myself. I choose to help empower you, not to own you nor possess you. I choose to love, honor, and respect you.

I will be as truthful and reliable as I can be. I will not agree to do things with you unless I truly want to, yet I will be respectful of, and sensitive to, your needs and feelings. When I want something from you, I will ask clearly, not hint or expect you to read my mind. I will not create expectations in my head concerning you or your actions then blame you for their unfulfillment. I will share my love, joy, and caring with you.

I will never use your words against you nor divulge your private thoughts and actions to others without your consent. I will communicate to you what "privacy" means

135

to me, and I will accept your definition of "privacy" for you. Any actions or words that relate to something the two of us said or did together should be considered private unless we have discussed it and agreed to reveal our actions or thoughts to others.

I will care for you when you are sick or hurt even if it means you want me to do nothing at all for you. I will respect that, in most instances, you know what is best for you, and what you need from me. However, I will not let you purposefully hurt or destroy yourself without attempting to persuade you otherwise. You may count on me for strength and emotional support when you are down and I expect the same of you.

We are separate and unique individuals who choose to enrich and cherish each other. Ultimately, though, only I can choose to be happy or not, fulfilled or not. I am equal to you, not more nor less. I will not compete with you and play "I win, you lose" games. I will enjoy your different qualities and work towards "win-win" situations. I feel proud of you and will not take you for granted. I will accept you as you are and not try to change those aspects of yourself I am uncomfortable with. I will endeavor to keep my mind open and my boundaries flexible. I will support your growth processes. I will not attack you in public or private when something occurs that I don't like. I will instead accept it as a part of who you are and rationally discuss it with you in private in order to more fully understand who you are. I will remember your love and constancy and communicate this to you. I will not judge you against my past relationships, good or bad. Nor will I hold on to issues or grudges. I will enjoy sharing hopes, dreams, and plans for the future with you now.

Our time together has a high priority in my life. I value our time and will make conscious efforts to ensure we have as much time for each other as we need. I also recognize that we need separate and alone time, too. I will respect your right to be apart from me, and I expect you to respect my right to have alone time also. I have friends and interests that are not in common with you; you also have friends and interests not in common with me. I will not be possessive or jealous of your time away from me, recognizing that the fulfillment and joy you receive benefits me as well. I will be open to uncommon experiences with you though. Our careers are also important to us and I will be understanding when job demands temporarily take a high priority in your life; I expect the same from you.

When problems occur, I will work with you to resolve them as soon as possible. When I am upset or conflicted, I will center myself, clarify my feelings, and determine my issues before confronting you. Only then will I approach you to discuss my issues. I will never make threats of breaking our commitments to each other, leaving you, or asking you to leave. I will never intentionally physically harm you nor threaten to. I will not expect either of us to be perfect. Occasionally I will get frustrated and stressed and disappointed, but I will not reject you nor attempt to control your individuality. I accept that I will have times of anger, sadness, fear, and pain and will want your emotional support. I will not feel you are attacking me when you express frustrations or bad feelings.

I use sexual intimacy as a way to express my love and inner self to you. I will not withhold sex to punish you nor use sex to control you. I value our sexual intimacy and will be open to your sexuality and need, as well as my own. I may not agree with every desire you have and I will be open to new experiences. However, I will not do things I am uncomfortable with, nor would I force you to do that which is uncomfortable for you. I will not be intimate with another unless you are comfortable with it. If you feel threatened, I will show you my love and reassure you and listen to you. However, I will not let you control my actions if you have unreasonable fears or a need to have power over me.

I will be responsible for supporting myself, and I will share what I can with you to the best of my abilities. I have personal property and I will respect and care for your personal property, as well as our common property, as if it were my own. I will make agreements with you concerning mutual financial matters. I will not control you with money, nor will I be controlled by your money. I also will consult with you before attempting to change our place of residence.

I commit myself to growing and changing and creating a conscious future with you. I will do my utmost to live up to the spirit of this agreement. We may revise or renegotiate this document as we deem suitable.

_____

Dated:_____, 20__
Witnessed by:_____

Books and Websites:

The Ethical Slut: A Guide to Infinite Sexual Possibilities by Easton, Dossie, and Liszt, Catherine A Publisher: Greenery Press (CA) Date Published: 1998 ISBN: 1890159018

Sex in History
by Tannahill, Reay
Publisher: Stein and Day
http://www.polyamorysociety.org/
http://www.swinglifestyle.com/
http://www.altplayground.net/
http://www.adultfriendfinder.com/

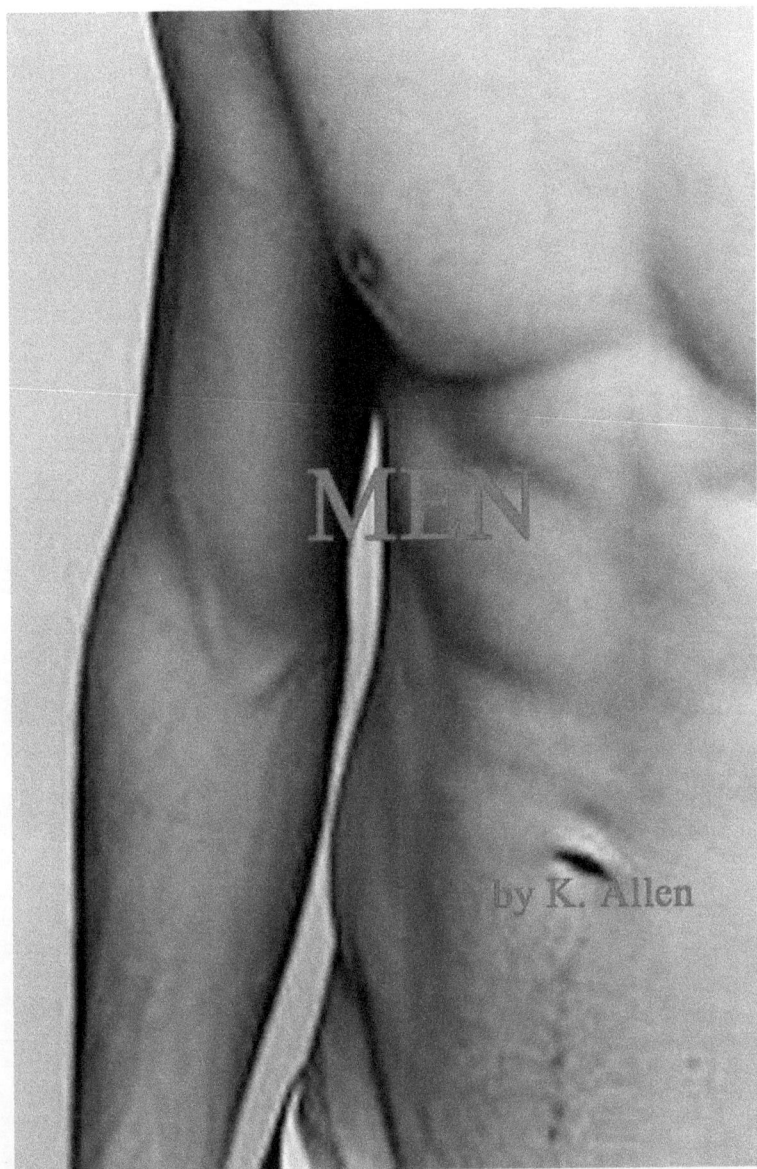

MEN

by K. Allen

by Corbis

Dedicated to
S. Steinberg
my very dear friend

Introduction

"if it has tires or testicles,
you're going to have trouble with it"

There are lots of men in the world. Some are more
delightful than others, but most will be very happy if only
you'd notice them. Men are neither monsters nor
simpletons; they are, like us, a mix of the good, the bad,
and the indifferent.

Men pretty much want the same things women want.
They mainly want someone to give a damn about them.
Men are human beings first and men second. This means
that men also have feelings, hopes, fears, dreams and
desires.

Men regard women as both the most fascinating and
the most exasperating people on the planet. To men,
women get upset at the silliest of things and women wonder
why they haven't strangled such unthinking persons yet.

This slender book is an effort at a kind of
reapproachment between the genders in the hope that more
women will have more fun and more men will remain
unstrangled.

The Basics

All fetuses begin as females. During pregnancy, sexual differentiation begins when the 'male to be' fetus receives a dose of testosterone. If this does not happen, the baby will appear female at birth and his masculinity will not emerge until puberty takes hold. Such a drastic change will have a profound effect. This is but the beginning of a male's perilous journey through life.

While men are physically stronger, they are biologically weaker than women. The Y chromosome is actually a fragment, leaving a male with no back up should anything be genetically wrong with him. Women, with their two X chromosomes, have a back-up should some genes be inoperable or damaged in some way. This differentiation means that males are more susceptible to illness, genetic maladies, and disease while allowing women to be carriers of defective genes and escape the malady. Men either have the disease or condition, or they don't.

Before the advent of DNA testing, there was little way of telling whether a child was the offspring of a particular man. The woman had to be there so it was easier to know if the child was hers. This leads to a basic psychological insecurity in men which leads to the jealousy and possessiveness we see in them. Some can overcome it, some cannot. Women can have it too but in their case it is based upon the fear of being abandoned and left to care for children on their own. If she has independent means, she has little cause to feel this way while money rarely cures a man of his jealousy and possessiveness.

These two emotions lead to aggressiveness and competitiveness. Not only must a man provide and hunt for his family, he must also protect and defend them. Other men represent a threat to his idea of the family unit. Then there are those disenfranchised men—those without homes or families. They do not have anything invested to hold them to the community and represent a threat to society at large. If they have no other outlet, they tend to turn to crime.

Thus genetically and behaviorally, men tend to live dangerously and to seek thrills more than women do. They like motorcycles, for example, more than women do. There's also another element to this matrix. They want women to notice them. They want women to think they are big and brave and therefore would make good husbands and fathers. Even if the women think they're idiots for doing something dangerous, men think it is worth the risk because "she noticed me". If a woman notices you, you've got a chance to mate with her. She might select you instead of the next guy.

Remember the peacock's tail? It is big, bold, flashy and a dreadful handicap to the bird. But if he manages to thrive in spite of the tail, the peahens know he has the goods! So the peahens mate with him and not the next bird whose tail is scrawny. In human society, this translates into having more wealth, a better job, and more and better goods than the next guy, assuming they are both decent men. Judgments in this area may be faulty, but generally speaking, that is what women consider first—can he provide for her and their children. The ability to protect and defend comes second. And why not? Seems a fair deal doesn't it?

It would be enough but we're human. Women would actually prefer to at least like the man they marry and have children with. They will have those children in their care for at least 18 years in our society. The relationship between the husband and wife has to last in order to accrue the maximum benefit. To accomplish this goal emotions and sex for pleasure, not just procreation enter the picture. This is also where the problems can start and take root. Throughout this period growth is taking place, not only in the children but in the parents as well. No one can predict or anticipate the outcome of this growth.

Why begin with sex? Because that's a males most basic and primary role. We could reproduce asexually and be a completely female society but the homogeny and sameness produced would not produce a world worth living in Men exist to provide genetic diversity. Every spermatozoon a male makes, approx 70 million of them each and everyday following puberty, is subtly different from every other spermatozoon he made, makes, or will make. Genes by their very nature are not stable. Within his testes the genes slip, slide, and jump along the chromosomes. Whole batches of code are written, edited, and rewritten in an ongoing genetic dance. He is even busy producing three kinds of spermatozoa, 'egg seekers', 'killers', and 'blockers'. The egg seekers role is to rush right off hunting for a waiting egg with the sole purpose of making more humans. The 'killers' however swim about seeking spermatozoa from competing males which they then try to kill off. The 'blockers' tangle their tails and form a wall trying to prevent spermatozoa from competitors entering the uterus. If he suspects his mate of dallying with other men, the proportion of his sperm will change and he will produce, quite subconsciously, more 'killers' and 'blockers' than he will egg-seekers.

Men take their job very seriously. Rather than seeing them as having 'sex on the brain', try to see them as being 'dedicated to their primary role'. They have to secure a mate, procreate effectively with her, provide and protect her during gestation when she is vulnerable, and then help raise the offspring to ensure that they live long enough to repeat the cycle making him a grandfather.

Men also have a secondary role to play. In order to do the above, they have to retain their female and not have her wandering off elsewhere. They may try to do this by force but if they are off with the guys hunting, well, they can not be in two places at once. Males have adapted and learned to amuse their partners, earn their respect, keep them well provided for and well protected. Basically, most males will try to keep her happy and content back at your cave. Sound familiar yet? Yes, there are men who just run about procreating without regard to the welfare of the women involved or the resultant children but when you consider this type of behavior, it becomes ludicrous. Without his protection and guidance anything could happen to his children. If his children do not survive to have healthy children of their own, he's been ineffective and inefficient, regardless of how much fun it might have been. At least, that's the theory in evolutionary terms. How does that play out in today's world?

Communication

Given that men generally exhibit higher levels of jealousy, possessiveness, competitiveness, and aggression, how do women cope? Usually, women are taught, in our society, to handle men through a mixture of denial and appeasement. We deny them what they want so they will respect us and appease them by trying to be tactful—to let them down easy, as the expression goes. We appease them so they will not give way to their emotions through frustration. Women fear that if men give way to their emotions, we will get hurt.

Yet women have similar drives and desires. While we want to fulfill them we feel we shouldn't, so when we try to be tactful, we also try to send out a message of hope. In doing this we send out 'mixed messages' to men and then wonder why men don't get it. Men want a straight yes or no, it is important for them to know where they stand. So when women, out of fear of being hurt, send out mixed messages, men become confused and irritated.

If you want to say something, just say it and say it like you mean it. Communicate to men without innuendo and without Meta messages or sub text. That's how women communicate with other women. That is not how you should communicate with men. Forget trying to appease them by leaving them some hope. Abandon fear and just speak. Some men might accuse you of being rude or arrogant, but you aren't being either, you are merely being clear.

Should a man exhibit his emotions beyond the level with which you are willing to endure them, he is not the man for you. If he does not exhibit the level of emotion you desire, once again, he is not the man for you. Changing him is not your job. Accept him as he is or don't. No more mixed messages, no more appeasement. You can apologize for your errors but you cannot accept responsibility for his errors or his emotions even if you are married to him.

Within our culture there are regional variations. You know what they are, you learned them in high school, but most men appreciate a straight forward woman. This is not a license to brutal; tactful speech as long as its meaning is clear, is always preferred.

Men use language differently than women do. If you listen to them when they are speaking among themselves you can learn these differences. Men change their speech when they speak to women because we demand that they do. We require them to 'mind their manners' most of the time. This means that men try to soften their message to prevent emotional storms. Women then tend to 'read into' what men tell them. Women search for hidden meanings rarely recognizing that men mean pretty much just what they said and nothing more.

So both genders pussyfoot around trying to avoid conflict and nothing is communicated. Men do have to mind their manners but women have to stop searching for hidden meanings. Men have to recognize the appeasement patterns in women's speech and not accept them but ask instead for a clear statement. "Remember, this is a man you're talking to." Men do not do 'nuance'.

Sub Societies

Men have their own sub society consisting of just other men which has its own rules. Women are not wanted nor are they allowed in. So don't try to enter it. You can, however, use it to your advantage by observing which men interact with which other men and how they do it. Mothers do this all of the time when they say "Talk to your son" to the boy's father. This is the age-old 'older male to younger male' counseling session. Then you find the younger males jousting with each other, trying to establish the pecking order within the group. Older men use more subtle methods but they do the same thing. Men feel more secure within a hierarchy so they seek to build one in every group. Do not interfere with this process.

Women have their own sub societies, some of which are hierarchies but most are not. Women tend to be in or out of the group rather than in a strict order within the group.

Part of the male social hierarchy is based upon sexual success—fulfillment of their primary role. More women, the best women, the most children, the most successful children, the better job, bigger portfolio, and so on—all of these become part of the 'social climbing'. The number one criterion is the ability to find and keep a high quality mate. Men realize that this can be difficult. Finding women is easy enough for most men, but finding high quality women can be difficult at times. Keeping a woman is the most difficult task of all with high quality women being more demanding and harder to keep.

What men mean by 'high-quality' is beauty, brains, wealth, charm, reproductive value, and that elusive ability to rock their world with only a glance. Since women have a limited period of time during which they are reproductive, younger women have a higher value than older women—that is to say, younger women have more time and chances to bear and raise more children. A female of 14 has a higher reproductive value than a female of 24 who has a higher reproductive value of a woman of 34 and so on until a woman hits menopause. This is just a fact. Fortunately, not all men want more children.

Each man will have his own priorities and those priorities will change over time. Each man has his own idea of beauty and this too will change over time as will yours. The young pup of 20-something looks very good to a 20-something woman but seems incredibly juvenile to a seasoned woman of 30-something.

As far as that elusive ability to rock their world with a single glance, most women have that capability if they'd only realize it. It begins with liking men. Sincerely liking men and everything about them from the way they smell to the way they think. If you feel comfortable around them, enjoy interacting with them, you're almost there. All you have to do now is learn to understand them and to acknowledge that yes, you do sincerely like and enjoy men.

Men like to be appreciated for what they do and for who they are. They want to have your respect and yes they care if you like them or not. They would really like it if you loved them. Try this now, just go up to your man and give him a big hug while saying something like "Love you, baby." That wasn't so hard was it? Of course it works better if you and he still love each other. If you have filed for divorce, or he has, it is too late and it is just best to move on.

There is one just more thing. Men need to be needed. They, like everyone, like to feel useful. It is part of that providing instinct they have. Letting them do things for you, instead of leaping up and doing them for yourself, will help fulfill this need. Always show some appreciation for their efforts; it is only polite after all.

Now that we've finished with the basics, it is time to explore some specifics.

Warning Signs

It is an unfortunate fact that the majority of women have suffered some kind of abuse at the hands of men at one time or another. While it is true that one person cannot know everything about another person, there are some things you can guess at with a fair degree of accuracy. If someone doesn't seem quite right, chances are that he isn't 'quite right'.

It is sometimes possible to predict the likelihood of the person you are currently or are about to become involved with of being abusive. Below are a list of behaviors and traits which are common in abusive personalities. These are commonly known as Warning Signs.

While not all abusive people show the same signs, or display the tendencies to the same extent, if you find that several behavioral traits are present, there is a strong tendency toward an abusive personality. Generally, the more signs presenting themselves, the greater the likelihood of violence. In some cases, an abuser may have only a couple of behavioral traits that can be recognized, but they are much exaggerated (e.g. extreme jealousy over ridiculous things).

Often the abuser will initially try to explain his/her behaviors as signs of his/her love and concern. This may flatter the victim at first, but as time goes on, the behaviors become more severe and serve to dominate, control and manipulate the victim.

Jealousy

At the beginning of a relationship, an abuser will always say that their jealousy is a sign of their love. He/she may question you about whom you have spoken to or seen during the day, may accuse you of flirting, or be jealous of time you spend with family, friends, children or hobbies which do not include him/her. As the jealousy progresses, he/she may call you frequently during the day or drop by unexpectedly. He/she may be unhappy about or refuse to let you work for fear you'll meet someone else, check the car mileage or ask friends to keep an eye on you. Jealousy is not proof of love; it is a sign of insecurity and possessiveness.

Controlling Behaviour

Controlling behaviour is often disguised or excused as concern. Concern for your safety, your emotional or mental health, the need to use your time well, or to make sensible decisions. Your abuser may be angry or upset if you are 'late' coming back from work, shopping, visiting friends, etc., even if you told him/her you would be back later than usual. Your abuser may question you closely about where you were, whom you spoke to, the context of every conversation you held, or why you did something he/she was not involved in. As this behaviour gets worse, you may not be allowed to make personal decisions about the house, clothing, going to church, how you spend your time, or money. You may even be made to ask for permission to leave the house or room. Alternately, he/she may theoretically allow you your own decisions, but penalize you for making the wrong ones. Concern for our loved ones to a certain extent is normal but trying to control their every move is not.

Quick Involvement

Many victims of abuse dated or knew their abuser for less than six months before they were engaged or living together. The abuser will often claim 'love at first sight', that you are 'made for each other', or that you are the only person whom he could ever talk to so openly, feel so at home with, could understand him so well. He/she may tell you that they have never loved anyone so much or felt so loved by anyone before; when in reality you have only known each other for a short amount of time. He/she needs someone desperately, and will pressure you to commit or make love before you feel the relationship has reached 'that stage'. He/she may also make you feel guilty for not committing yourself to him/her.

Unrealistic Expectations

The abuser may expect you to be the perfect husband, wife, mother, father, lover, and friend. He/she is very dependent on you for all his/her needs, and may tell you he/she can fulfill all your needs as lover, friend, and companion. Statements such as: "If you love me", "I'm all you need.", and "'You are all I need." are common. Your abuser may expect you to provide everything for him/her emotionally, practically, financially or spiritually, and then blame you for not being perfect or living up to expectations.

Isolation

The abuser may try to curtail your social interaction. He/she may try to prevent you from spending time with your friends or family and demand that you only go places 'together'. He/she may accuse you of being 'tied to your mother's apron strings', 'not committed to the relationship', or view people who are your personal friends as 'causing trouble' or 'trying to put a wedge' between you. He/she may want to live in the country without a phone, not let you use the car, stop you from working, furthering your education, or qualifications.

Blame-shifting for Problems

Very rarely will an abusive personality accept responsibility for any negative situation or problem. If they are unemployed, can't hold down a job, were thrown out of college or University, or fall out with their family, it is always someone else's fault. The blame always falls somewhere else, be it the boss, the government, or their mother. They may feel that someone is always doing them wrong, or out to get them. He/she may make mistakes and then blame you for upsetting him/her or preventing him/her from doing as they wished to do.

Blame-shifting for Feelings

The abuser will deny that any feelings stem from within him/her. He/she will see these feelings as reactions to your behaviour or attitude toward him/her. He/she may say things such as; 'you make me mad', 'you're hurting me by not doing what I ask', or that he/she cannot help feeling mad, upset, etc. Feelings may be used to manipulate you, i.e. 'I would not be angry if you didn't ...' Positive emotions will often also be seen as originating outside the abuser, but are more difficult to detect. Statements such as 'You make me happy' or 'You make me feel good about myself' are also signs that the abuser feels you are responsible for his/her sense of well-being. Either way, in his/her mind you become the cause of all feelings both good and bad. Therefore transferring responsibility for his/her emotional well-being and happiness. Consequently, you are also to blame for any negative feelings such as anger, upset or depression.

Hypersensitivity

Most abusers have very low self-esteem and are therefore easily insulted or upset. They may claim their feelings are 'hurt' when they are really angry, or take unrelated comments as personal attacks. They may perceive normal setbacks (having to work additional hours, being asked to help out, receiving a parking fine, etc.) as grave personal injustices. They may view your preference for something which differs from their own as a criticism of their taste and therefore themselves (e.g., blue wallpaper rather than pink, etc.).

Cruelty to Animals

The abuser may punish animals brutally, be insensitive to their pain or suffering, or neglect to care for them to the point of cruelty. Examples being: not feeding them all day or leaving them in areas he/she knows will cause them suffering or distress. There is a strong correlation between cruelty to animals and domestic violence which is still being researched.

Cruelty to Children

The abusers unrealistic expectations of their partner are often mirrored in their attitude toward children. He/she will think of children as 'small adults' and blame the children for not being responsible, having common sense, or understanding. He/she may expect children to be capable of things far beyond their ability (e.g. is angry with a two-year old for wetting their pants or being sick on the carpet, waking at night or being upset by nightmares) and will often meet out punishments for 'naughtiness' the child could not be aware of. Abusers may tease children until they cry, or punish them much further than what is deemed appropriate. He/she may not want children to eat at the table, expect them to stay quiet, or keep to their room all evening while he/she is at home. Since abusers want all your attention focused on themselves, they resent your spending time with the children or any normal demands and needs the children may have. As mentioned previously,(cruelty to animals), there is a very strong link between Domestic Violence and Child Abuse.

'Playful' use of Force in Sex

He/she may pressure you to agree to forceful or violent acts during sex, or want to act out fantasies in which you are helpless. A male abuser may let you know that the idea of "rape" excites him. He/she may show little concern about whether you want to have intercourse or not and can use sulking or anger to manipulate you into compliance. Initiating sexual activities while you are sleeping, demanding sex when you are ill or tired, or refusing any form of intimacy unless you are willing to go 'all the way', can all be signs that he/she may be sexually abusive or sexually violent. This could lead to forcing you into sexual behaviors and situations with which you may be uncomfortable.

Rigid Sex Roles

Abusers usually believe in stereotypical gender roles. A man may expect a woman to serve him, stay at home, and obey him in all things— even to the point of criminal behaviors. A male abuser will often see females as inferior to males, less intelligent, and incapable of living as a whole person without being in a relationship. Female abusers may expect the man to provide for them entirely, shifting the responsibility for her well-being onto him, or heckle him as 'not being a real man' if he shows any interpreted weakness or emotion.

Verbal Abuse

In addition abusers tend to say things that are meant to be cruel and hurtful, which they will do in public or private setting. This type of abuse can include degrading remarks, belittling comments, and trivializing accomplishments. Often the abuser will tell you that you are 'stupid and could not manage without him/her. He/she may keep you up all night to "sort this out once and for all" or even wake you at night to continue his/her verbal assault. The abuser may say kind things to your face, but speak badly about you to friends and family.

Dr. Jekyll and Mr. Hyde

Very rarely do abusers conform to the stereotypical image of a constantly harsh, nasty or violent person, either in public or private. More frequently the abuser portrays a perfectly normal and pleasant facade to the outside world (often they have responsible jobs or are respected and important members of the local community or Church) while reserving the abuse for the privacy of your own home. The opposite is equally as true, abusers are not always overtly abusive or cruel, but can display apparent kindness and consideration when they deem it necessary. This Jekyll and Hyde tendency of the abuser serves to further confuse the victim, while protecting themselves from any form of outside suspicion. Many victims describe "sudden" mood swings such as one minute nice and the next explosive or hysterical, or one minute happy and the next minute sad. This does not indicate some special "mental problem" but is typical of abusive personalities, and can be related to other secondary characteristics such as hypersensitivity.

Drink or Substance Abuse

While neither drinking nor the use of drugs are signs of an abusive personality, heavy drinking or drug abuse may be a warning sign as well as increase the risks of abuse, especially physical violence. Often an abusive person will blame the drink for his/her abuse. However, a person who, knowing there is a risk he/she could be violent when drinking or on drugs, chooses to get drunk or high, is in effect, choosing to abuse. The link between substance abuse and domestic abuse is still being researched, and it is apparent that while neither alcohol nor drugs necessarily cause violence, they do increase the risk of violence.

History of Battering or Sexual Violence

Very rarely is abuse or violence a one-off event: a batterer will beat any woman he is with; a sexually abusive person will be abusive toward all his intimate partners. Situational circumstances do not make a person an abusive personality. Sometimes friends or family may try to warn you about the abuser or the abuser themselves may tell you that he/she has hit or sexually assaulted someone in the past. They may further go on to explain that "he/she made me do it by ..." or in some other shift the responsibility and blame on to the victim. They may tell you that it won't happen with you because "you love them enough to prevent it" or "you won't be stupid enough to wind me up that much". Once again, this is denying ones own responsibility for the abuse, and shifting the responsibility for the relationship to remain abuse-free on to you. Past violence is one of the strongest indicators that abuse will occur.

Threatening Violence

This would obviously include any threat of physical harm such as "If you speak to him/her again, I'll kill you", or "If any wife of mine acted like John's did, I'd give her a right seeing to". But can also include less obvious psychological threats, such as "If you leave me, I will kill myself". Threats are designed to manipulate and control you, to keep you in your place, and to prevent you from making your own decisions. Most people do not threaten their mates, but an abuser will excuse this behaviour using one or more of the following rationales: "everybody talks like that" maintaining that he/she is only saying this because the relationship and or you are so important to him/her, telling you that you are "over-sensitive" for being upset by such threats, or obviously you want to hurt him/her.

Breaking or Striking Objects

The abusive person may break your treasured object, beat his/her fists on the table or chair or throw something at or past you. Breaking your things is often used as a punishment for some imagined misdeed on your part. Sometimes it will be justified by saying that now that you are with him/her, you don't need these items any more. Breaking your possessions also has the effect of de-personalizing you, denying you your individuality or literally trying to break links to your past. Beating items of furniture or throwing objects will often be justified by saying you pushed him/her so far that they lost control. Once again on the surface an example of shifting the blame for this behaviour on to you, but in reality it is used to terrorize you into submission. Only very immature or abusive people beat on objects in the presence of other people in an effort to threaten or intimidate them.

Any Force during an Argument

An abuser may physically restrain you from leaving the room, lash out at you with his/her hand or another object, pin you against a wall or shout 'right in your face'. Basically any form of force used during an argument can be a sign that actual violence is a strong possibility.

Regardless of which side of this equation you are on— get immediate help NOW! There is no future in this kind of relationship. You will not change either him/her or yourself. It is in your best interest to just leave and file a police report. Any sign of gentleness on your part will only be seen as 'weakness' by him/her and he/she will continue to press, berate and badger you into coming back to him/her for more abuse. Just be done with him/her. If you are the abuser—get help. There is something seriously wrong with you that only a medical professional can help you resolve.

There are women who do dreadful things because they think they'll hold onto their man by doing them. They need professional medical help as well. Women should not get off 'scot-free' but 'sisterhood' means looking after one another and helping where we can.

On to more pleasant topics!

We shall begin with flirting or 'how to hold onto a man while keeping him at arm's length'. The rule here is, 'do not touch him'. If you touch him, even lightly on his hand, he may take that as sexual interest in him and as permission to touch you. This is fine if that's where you want to go, but it isn't 'keeping him at arm's length'. So long as you don't touch him, you can chat, laugh at his jokes, tell a few of your own and so on—it remains just flirting.

Under the heading of flirting with sexual intent are two games: "Confuse-a-Male" and "Shot Your Fox." Both are extremely feminine and as such they both entrance and exasperate men. By using "Confuse-a-Male" you are indicating a moderate level of interest in him. "Shot Your Fox" is used when you plan on bedding him at the earliest opportunity, provided he doesn't make a mistake.

"Confuse-a-Male" is where you pull out all the stops and use elliptical references, innuendo, and nuance to the maximum extent permitted by law. Go ahead and verbally tease him and run linguistic rings around him—if you can.

An experienced man will know what you are doing, and what it means (he may even play along) while an inexperienced man will just be befuddled.

"Shot Your Fox" is when both the man and the woman slyly, elaborately, and with great deliberation refuse to get each other's jokes while playing one joke off another in a kind of stately dance. This can only be done with a man who is capable of playing it. The first one who laughs, loses the game. Once again, an experienced man will understand exactly what you are doing and what your intentions are while the inexperienced man will undoubtedly make a mistake.

Men expect women to exhibit some sibylline behavior so not being straight-forward is okay, but only to a point. Some shyness, indecisiveness, and even timidity are accept-able but again, only up to a point. Once you get to know him and he has earned a measure of your trust, he expects you to calm down and relax. The time has then come for you to 'step up' and enter a relationship or to 'step off' and decline his offer of a relationship.

Male Anatomy

Since you are familiar with most of his body, I will focus upon just one area, the male G-Spot.

Male Reproductive Tract

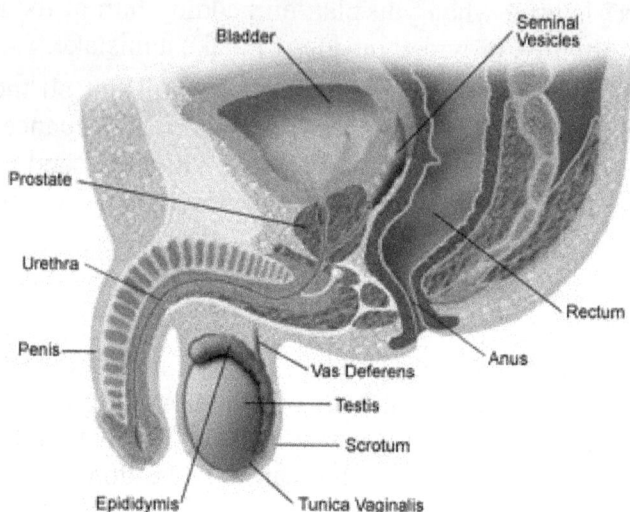

Quite simply, the Male G-Spot is the prostate, or more specifically, the prostate-perineum. What are they? The prostate is the male prostate gland, and the perineum is a dime-sized soft spot between the anus and scrotum. The important nerves that control the sexual organs, including those controlling erection, orgasm, and ejaculation, converge at the prostate and the perineum area. This means that this area is essentially a man's "command center" for sexual pleasure. The tissue that forms the urethral sponge, or G-spot, in female anatomy forms the prostate, which you can think of as the male G-spot (or the "P-spot") in male anatomy. Gently caressing this gland by hand or with a toy made for this greatly enhances the intensity of his orgasm. Enjoying such play does not have anything to do with his sexual orientation.

Relationships

There are several varieties of relationships available. You can choose between open or closed, serious or not serious or the 'friends with benefits' arrangement that is currently popular. Which ever you choose, he must agree with it or the relationship is over before it has begun. If he wants something different and negotiation is not possible, then just say goodbye.

Within a relationship, of any kind, fair is fair and communication is key. This means if you want him to do this, you had better be prepared to do that. Talk with him not at him. Listen to him without looking for hidden meanings or defensively filtering his message. The 'silent treatment' and the 'using sex as a reward' treatment are childish games and any use of them immediately diminishes your credibility.

Whatever your past has been, focus your attention on this man, right here, right now. He should not have to pay for others past crimes. Neither of you is solely responsible for the future of this relationship, it is a partnership and team effort. No 'future thinking'. If you cannot talk about issues sensibly as an adult, they were not important, so you drop it, or you are too close to them and need more time to think them through. There is no such thing as 'making up', there is only problem resolution.

Disagreements during the early stages of a relationship are to be expected as you grow used to each other and define the boundaries of your relationship. Fights are not acceptable. Be civil, sincere, and respectful when discussing your issues.

The Cult of Virginity

Nothing has ruined more relationships than this idea of virginity having value. There was a reason for this before reliable birth control, but even then, the main idea behind it was repugnant. The cult of virginity was founded on the belief that once a woman had sex with a man she was 'tainted' and had no further value. None, not even as a human being with a brain and whatever talent she may possess. Girls were subjected to wedding nights that resembled rapes and were considered sluts if they showed the least desire or enjoyment, even within marriage.

Ignorance of your most basic human drive is not a 'gift' and there's nothing 'precious' about virginity. Without some experience with men, and with yourself, your chances of selecting the most suitable husband are slender. Consider that the number one complaint of married men after 20 years with the same woman is lack of sex. Why is that?

It is because women have the idea that being sexually experienced, enjoying sex and desiring masculine attention makes them a worthless slut. They pretend before marriage and then give it all up once they've had their children, if they even have children.

The truth is that women have the same desires as men do. If she manages it properly, she can have a satisfying, safe, and entirely electrifyingly enjoyable sex life before, during, and after marriage—for her entire life. A sexually self-aware woman has the capacity to 'out-gun' any six men you'd care to name. Focus that kind of attention upon a man and he'd be more than just merely delighted. Show him what you like, tell him what you like, participate fully, reciprocate, initiate sex, take control—have fun with this! How can you do all that if you have no idea what you like and what you're doing?

Furthermore, each man has his own style as well as his own issues when it comes to sex. The more men you enjoy, the more you learn, the better your choices become, and the less you fear. The 'sacredness' of sex lies not in the sex itself but in the bond between the partners.

The proper management of sexual contact includes all parties using some form of birth control. The Pill is the most effective for women, and the use of condoms greatly prevents the transmission of any diseases and generally makes clean-up easier. As for the rest, men will always offer their services, but in reality, you always have the final say not only as to enjoying him or not, but even as to how you will enjoy him—the individual acts themselves. The woman controls the action. Just remember that 'fair is fair'.

However, there is nothing more pathetic than a woman chasing after or mooning over a man who is not interested in her or doesn't want her. If he doesn't 'step up' then it is time for you to 'step off'. That is, to move on and find another. There are lots of men out there and all of them are potentially interested in you. If he wants to be with you, he will be with you. He will make himself available. If he doesn't then he isn't interested in you.

Next in line is the woman who stays with an unsatisfactory man because that's all she thinks she can get or keep. If he proves to be unsatisfactory, it is time to move on. Just say goodbye and walk away without fuss and no looking back. There are other men out there.

Breaking Up

All terminations of must be done in person and in an up front, straight forward manner. Regardless of who is kicking whom out—the result should be a quiet and orderly separation. He said/she said recriminations just lead to a downward spiral of tit-for-tat snipings which benefit no one and make you look like a bitter old hag, and who needs that? Be firm, be non-confrontational, but don't back down. There is nothing good or easy about saying goodbye but that does not mean either of you are permitted a pound of flesh in retribution.

Divorce is another matter. Everything depends on the reason for the separation and how well you communicate. If this is a mutual termination then things can be done together and in a civil and adult manor. If he has caused the demise of the relationship and there is no hope of civility, then get yourself the divorce lawyer with the longest fangs and make him/her work for his/her pay. Have no contact or further conversations with your soon-to-be-ex husband; do everything through you lawyer. Consult your financial advisor about what settlements would be the most advantageous to you and yet reasonably equitable to both parties considering the circumstances. If the two of you have children together, always remember that both of you will always remain the parents of your children, and regardless of who gets custody, the children will miss the non-custodial parent. Whatever else, behave like an adult.

He left you for a younger woman?

Thank god she came along when she did! You have been trying to unload this man for years but since he'd never survive on his own you just couldn't bring yourself to throw him out into the street. So thank the poor woman for her help and wish her the best of luck! And say it with a huge grin!

Swinging

It may surprise you to learn that in this lifestyle, woman rule all. However women come to the lifestyle, once they are there, they find it liberating! They can give up worrying that they aren't slim enough, they aren't pretty enough, they're not young enough, or they're not sexy enough. They can give up apologizing for their desires, their likes, or their dislikes. They can stop being a 'good girl', give modesty a rest, and live out their fantasies to their heart's content.

There is a difference between love, lust, and sexual congress. Many couples form lasting friendships with other couples within the lifestyle. Most 'playing couples' find that their marital relationships deepen and become richer through sharing with others.

There are however, as in all things, ground rules. Whatever you and your husband decide those rules are, each party must abide by them until those rules are changed by mutual negotiation.

If you are at all jealous, you'll have to get over it. If you cannot trust your husband, or he you, or if either of you doubts the strength of your bond, this is not the lifestyle for you. Either you give up the lifestyle together or you sever the relationship.

Age Differences

Younger men with older women or older men with younger women; both kinds of relationships will come under society's fire because society does not like even the appearance of possible exploitation. If you both can handle the stress then go for it so long as you both are 'legal'.

Younger men tend to have zest, energy, and potential but no real skill. They are at the height of their fertility and at the bottom rung of their careers. They have neither money nor history. They also have a kind of masculine vanity that appears as bravado and hubris. Young men are usually rather reckless and unthinking. He might also be a virgin or somewhat shy about initiating sex. Those who are diffident may suddenly leap without looking fearing that if they look, they will not leap and will have another missed opportunity on their record.

Older men have skill, conversation, money, history, and usually wives. If you are at all serious about wanting a relationship with an older man, you must first find one without a wife. You do not want a man who will lie to you. Sincerity is mandatory. Dallying with a married man is more complicated and he will not leave his wife so there's little to be gained by it but it remains a choice since he cannot get attached and he has to go home.

But older men have experience and they know what they want. If they want children, they will look for a reproductive woman. Older men will also have their issues, usually focused upon physical issues such as knees, backs, and erectile dysfunction. But there are issues brought on by their life experiences. You have your issues and so have they. Older men are most certainly not virgins. If you find one, run rapidly away. If not one woman in all of his years has found him 'acceptable', chances are you also will not.

Shyness and unconfident men need to relax. You can do this by being less aggressive and talking. Ask him questions. Set him at ease without totally blanking out all sexual interest. Take the relationship slowly and comfortably. Ask him to help you with things he's good at and you aren't. Be calm and gentle without being a total doormat or a timid little mouse. Never ever use the word 'friends' to describe your relationship! To men 'friends' equals doom! Men want lovers not female friends.

And why not? Knowing that you are important to another person is a very happy experience! It is pleasure and pleasure is good for you! Those within loving relationship of all varieties live longer, healthier, and happier lives. There is nothing wrong with that!

Finding Men

If you have a clear idea of the kind of man you want, you will have an idea where you will find him and what you should do to capture his initial interest. Like calls to like. Therefore, if you wish a higher quality man, you will have to be of higher quality yourself and go where such men are to be found. This does not mean that you have to be someone you aren't; it means you have to be your best self with an upgraded, more chic, and more appropriate style. Make your chosen 'hunting ground' an activity you sincerely enjoy that happens to have a great number of male participants. Take lessons. Have your relatives and friends introduce you around. Do charity work. You will not find him if you're sitting at home.

Common Myths

1. Men Have Sex on The Brain. Yes and no. It is their primary function but no, they think about other things as well. They aren't machines.

2. Men Only Want One Thing. Not any more than you do. Men want a variety of things. Mostly they want you to care about them.

3. Men Want Virgins/Younger Women. Some men might but most actually don't want either. Fully 80% of married men are perfectly happy in their current relationships.

4. Older Women Have No Chance. Not at all true! A woman of any age has a decent chance of finding a suitable man, if she remains open to the possibility.

5. Older Men Are Creepy. Older men have more skill, more patience, and are much more fun than younger men who still have much to learn.

6. Men Can Have Children At Any Age. Yes it can happen but men too have a decreasing fertility as they age. So while it is possible it becomes less likely.

7. Jealousy is Natural. Jealousy is based upon fear not love and is therefore only for losers.

8. Any Man is Better Than No Man. Also not true. If you have skills, and are sensible, you can make it on your own.

9. You can judge the size of a man's penis by the size of his feet, or hands, etc. Not at all true! There is absolutely NO correlation between the size of a man's appendages and the size of his penis. The average size is 5 to 8" long and 2 to 4" around.

Basically, if the sentence begins "Men are…" you can discount it. All one can say is that some men are and some men aren't.

Conclusion

I hope that this helps increase your understanding of men. Men are wonderful people as are women. That being said, do not get lax during your relationships. Taking him for granted, being difficult to live with, always being argumentative, not finishing what you start, and generally being a pain will kill any relationship. Learn to effectively communicate and keep on communicating. Having a home with a loving partner as your 'safe haven' is not so terrible after all. Now get out there!

Love as you live – unstintingly!

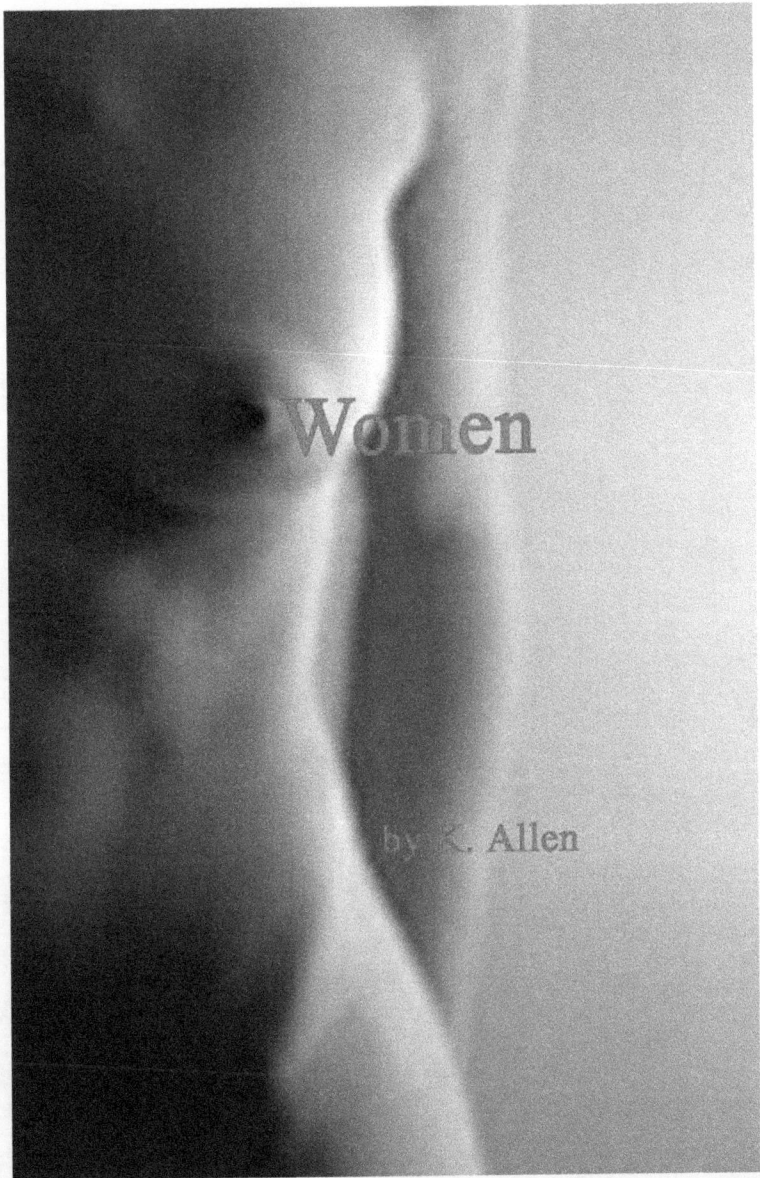

Women

by R. Allen

by Corbis

Dedicated
to
J. S. Zupan
and
Camden C. Cochran

Introduction

It is a testament to the essential kindness of women that most men remain unstrangled. This small primer has been written by an independent woman of vast interpersonal experience in the hopes that men will remain unstrangled because they... finally... 'get it'.

The Basics

There are lots of women in this world. All of them are potentially interested in you. We are neither goddesses to be worshipped nor members of some alien species to be feared. We are people much like yourselves—good, bad, and indifferent in a marvelous mix unique to each individual.

Women have, however, been educated differently than you have. Women tend to regard men as potentially hostile and untrustworthy idiots. Women are often seen as 'prey' to some men and this tends to influence their thoughts and behaviors. Just imagine how irritated you would be if unsuitable men kept pestering you. If she says "No" then, dammit, she means "No"! She does not mean "Maybe", or "Next week". If she changes her mind later, that is her business and the message has to come directly from her. She'll let you know. Women have also been regarded as beautiful idiots by some men so when men presume to tell someone they have never met 'what she needs', well, the resulting conversation is not going to go well.

When preparing to date, a man usually does not have to wonder if he'll end up dead in a ditch somewhere. Women do. She may look and act all big, bad, and bold; but she knows the risks are very real. Your first mission is to learn that while you are out for a good time—she's out to make it home alive and in one piece. Having a good time would be, for her, perhaps too much to hope for. All she is hoping is that it will not be a bad time. You have to be non-threatening to her from the outset. The bigger you are, relative to her, the more you're going to have to work at it. Be calm, cool, collected, and have excellent manners without being at all shy, indecisive, or timid.

We do not like shy, timid, indecisive men. How can we rely upon you if you are any of those? Even the most independent woman wants to know her man is capable of being there for her should she need him. If she asks you to order her food for her, do so after asking if there's anything she cannot eat. The answer to "What do you want to do? is never "I don't know". If you're at a loss, pick up some take out, drive to someplace nice and have a moonlight picnic. Do anything but say "I don't know".

Be prepared to talk and to listen. Watch her body language. Maintain eye contact and smile. Stay close without looming over her. Do not touch her until she touches you. Ask for her name and number and/or email address but do not make any promises you are not prepared to keep—ever. Remember that you are being trustworthy.

You will notice that I have omitted admonitions to get fit and dress well. Some women do care about your appearance, of course, but most will be more than happy to take you as you are as long as you are clean and cute. I, myself, have a special fondness for tall, furry, somewhat rounded men in their 40's and by tall I mean taller than me when I'm not wearing high heels. Most women have just such a secret preference when it comes to men. This preference comes out instantly and it acts like a magnet.

"No, it isn't anything about what he looks like etc, etc, etc.—it is the vibe that came off of him. Perhaps it is pheromones? It happens so very rarely but somehow the man just SPEAKS to me and I am powerless to resist! I MUST HAVE HIM NOW!!!"

So get out there and mingle about. Give the lady a chance to spot you.

Above a certain age, being a virgin will make women run screaming from you out into the night even if there are axe murderers out there waiting for her. Some women are into educating the young but most are not. A woman preparing to throw herself into your arms wants to know that you know what to do with her when you catch her. If she mentions whips and chains and your eyes don't light up, you may have a problem. However you choose to gain experience, get some. There is no need to tell her about it however. She will know.

We all have our insecurities but you don't want to show yours. If you show yourself to be other than calm and in control, you will lose the woman. An air of confidence, of social poise is needed to win her. Never create a scene and especially never create a scene in public. No matter how rowdy it gets, do not get rowdy yourself. If you use the wrong fork, no matter, just quietly use the other one during the next course. Being able to quietly go along as if nothing had ever happened is an asset in her eyes. No one wants a man who is prone to going off the deep end at the slightest provocation. You're too big a man to be put out of your stride by such small things anyway, right?

This may sound odd, but be prepared to turn her down nicely. If the lady of the moment is flaky, drunk, or otherwise not to your taste, or if what she proposes is not what you want to do, you will have to say no to her. If you do not want her unbuttoning your shirt buttons, just hold her hands and lean in to whisper "Not here" in her ear. If you reject her nicely, she will not hold it against you. Being able to say no nicely will only enhance your image as a calm, and in control, man among men.

Learn to flirt and to love flirting. You want a light, witty way with words. Women like intelligent men. Being able to slide in a sly joke, being able to appreciate it when she slides in a sly joke, is good. Only leave the malicious jokes at home. There is to be no bashing of anyone here. Let her see that you enjoy being with her and that your brain is fully operational, thank you. This also shows that you can be kind.

Tell her she looks charming, delicious, whatever but say something to show her that she interests you physically as well. Do not get grabby or back her into a corner. Don't get creepy about this. Have the courage to be sincere, good-tempered, and honest with her. Hidden agendas are not permitted. Yes, she wants a good time as well but that's after she assured of making it home safe and sound.

Teasing lightly is fine but 'busting' on her is not permitted. Only after she has bedded you will she permit you to 'bust' her and even then be careful with it. She is not like your buddies. Women expect men to be exasperating but only up to a point. If she feels that you are being at all juvenile, she'll walk away. She wants a grown man, not a little boy dressed up in a 'man suit'. Be juvenile and you will lose all of your credibility.

To sum up clearly, 'grow a set' but keep your head on straight and your heart in the right place.

Young Men

Tone it down, buddy, and stop waving it in her face. Back off a bit, you're crowding her. Remember first and foremost that she can buy bigger, easier to handle than you, and it will last as long as the supply of batteries holds out. You have got to bring more than that to the table or it is no deal.

Learn to listen. Younger women might enjoy toying with you by playing coy. Refuse to play. Turn your attention elsewhere. Be civil but not friendly. Don't say things like "Well, if you're not interested...". Just quietly become absent. Smile, nod, and move on. Refuse to communicate. If she wants you, she'll have to step up to the plate to get you. If she wants you; she will—don't worry.

There's nothing coy about an older woman, most of who will, figuratively speaking, pat you on the head and send you out to play elsewhere. Of course if you do run across a true full-blooded cougar, you are easy meat. Young men are defenseless against her. Enjoy the ride and the education. Just learn to say "Yes, ma'am" with a smile.

Ask questions and then listen to what she says. Practice this by talking to women without trying to pick them up. Any woman, anywhere, has a history, has interests, and has ideas. What are hers? What does she think of the Celtics? Does she think the rain will clear before nightfall? What does she fancy will win the fourth race at Aqueduct? The point is to get comfortable approaching, talking, and listening to women as people. This is not the time to flirt.

Do you have a life? How can you ask someone to share it, even if only temporarily, if you don't have one? Do you have interests, a history, a career, relatives, or hobbies? Remember, you have to bring more than just wild and not terribly skilled sex to the negotiating table. Get a life and bring that along too.

Men in Uniform

The kind of uniform does matter. Anything military wins hands down. Law enforcement and firefighters come next in line. Any other uniform is beside the point. Why do women like men in uniform? They like it because these men have shouldered the burdens associated with that uniform. They have 'stepped up'. If he has attained any rank at all, then he has learned self control, discipline, and has a measure of leadership. He has also learned tactics and how to focus upon the mission both of which are very effective when dating. He also has stories to tell. It is an unfair advantage to be sure, but you may luck out and he'll be a macho jerk. It can happen.

Men with Wealth

The only thing better than a uniform is wealth. I am speaking of real money; the kind that comes in portfolios, statements of holdings, and of his family's portraits on the paper currency or the family's name on large multi-national corporations or foundations. A tricked out and souped up Honda Accord is not real money. Real 'bling' earns interest and pays dividends. Wealth of this kind means security to women. Allying herself to such a family secures her children's future from want, usually. But he could be a jerk too, so hang in there. For the rest of us, wealth is usually gained through remunerative employment, saving, and investing or in making a success out of your own business, all of which require work. A man who works gains credibility and respect. A man, who works effectively and doesn't waste his paycheck, earns even more respect. Working women especially appreciate a working man. They view him as a team player. If you can't hold a job, they do not want to know you. Get gainfully employed and get your finances in order.

Older Men

Have more money, more skill, more experience, and more issues than younger men. They also have a more complicated life and bigger and better toys. Except for one issue, they can out-compete the younger men without too much effort. That issue is the visceral rejection factor contained in the statement "you're old enough to be my father".

This is only an issue with young women who view men beyond a certain age as being dirty old men. If you aren't hunting them, then it is not an issue for you. If you are after young women then I am sorry to say it, but you're going to have an uphill fight on your hands. This kind of rejection is almost impossible to overcome. If you receive it, just smile, nod, and move on.

The best tactic for older men is to mingle, chat, and look for evidence of interest from women. Wait for it. Once she has signaled that she's interested, then move in without fuss, and set her at ease by talking with her. You've dated women before. You'll date women again later on. There's no rush and no pressure here so you can relax and enjoy her company. Displaying this kind of confidence will only spark her interest.

Do not bring up your past. Do not be bitter about your ex should you have one. Focus upon this woman, right here, right now. Have no expectations and make no demands. Get her name, her number, and her email address but make no promises. Do not complain. Women tend to see complaining as whining. Do not fuss. If you do, you will remind her of her aged maiden aunts. Instant loss of credibility.

Examples

Picture in your mind how these three men appeared to the women they dated. Man number one took her to lunch and then complained to the waiter about the state of the silverware, then quizzed him about the menu and then about the various kinds of beer on offer, while she's sitting there waiting for him to pay some attention to her. The waiter left and he continued to complain about this and that to the lady. The food wasn't quite right. The beer wasn't quite as described. This place charges too much too.

Man number two went rather well through lunch and then leaned back in his chair and informed the lady that since he had driven several hours to meet her for lunch that she owed him at least a blowjob in the parking lot as a reward for his effort. The lady, being a lady, met this demand with silence, placed a twenty on the table, and left him flat right then and there without saying another word to him.

The dinner date went well. She was reasonably pleased as she drove him to his car several blocks away. During the drive he literally attacked her in her own car. Fortunately it was summer and she had the windows open. Also fortunately there were construction workers nearby who heard her screams and headed for her car. The man ran away. She got out of there with a hairline fracture of her right cheekbone from his fist.

All of these men were old enough to know better. The ladies were not interested in why these men behaved as they did and their reasons do not really matter. Each of these men stupidly and blatantly disqualified themselves. One of the women, the one who dated the complainer, was philosophical about it but the others, especially the lady who was attacked, were more than ready to damn the entire male sex to the deepest pit in hell for eternity. In other words, don't make it harder for the next man.

184

Men of this age usually are looking for some kind of a relationship. If this is true in your case, then be clear exactly what kind of relationship you are looking for and for how long. Be clear about what quality or qualities in a woman you consider the most important. You do not need to spell this out to every woman you meet but if you're serious then she should have a good idea of where she stands. Whatever you do, play fairly. Demanding that she be exclusive while leaving you free to play the field, or vice versa, doesn't work.

Jealousy/Possessiveness

Rid yourself of it, period. Being jealous doesn't work and will only get worse over time. If she's jealous or possessive, say goodbye to her. No one needs that kind of drama in their life. Do not make the mistake of thinking that jealousy equals love because it doesn't. Jealousy means distrust. You do not trust her, you do not trust yourself, and you do not trust in the strength of your relationship if you are jealous; mainly because you do not think yourself worthy of her and the equal of any other man out there. Jealousy is for losers. Jealousy is a sign of weakness. Jealousy is a red flag, that you're neither safe nor fun to be with. Women want to stay with men out of love not out of fear that he'll go off the deep end.

Violence

Never raise your hand to a woman in anger. Never permit a woman to raise her hand to you in anger. Being this out of control indicates an urgent need for professional medical attention. This is also illegal and will involve law enforcement and the judicial system. I am very sorry to say that the majority of women have suffered abuse of one kind or another at the hands of men. A few men have shared this fate as well. This is the main reason why women regard men as little more than untrustworthy brutes and this is why you must be non-threatening if you ever want to get close to a woman. Do not ask her about her past unless you are prepared for the answer. It will not be a pretty tale.

This is not to be confused with alternative play.

Agendas

Most people go out dating or hunting with a plan in mind, an agenda, and this is fine up to a point. One should always be prepared to jettison the plan should an excellent opportunity arise. While looking for Ms. Right you can occasionally stop to play with Ms. Wrong.

The problem with agendas is not matching the hunting grounds with the sort of woman you're seeking. Ms. Devout's not hanging out at the clubs with the swinging set. The next problem is what happens when she doesn't stick to the script you've laid out in your mind? You have decided that women take a long time to warm up and that they want a man to make the moves and here comes a sexually aggressive lady who is more than willing to jump your bones without even waiting to say hello first. It pays to be somewhat flexible when it comes to agendas.

Femme-Speak

Women use a more nuanced language than men use. Women like to speak using elliptical references. Women enjoy digging into the heart of topics including motives, speculation and the topic's mother's third cousin's maiden aunts' paternal ancestors to the third generation's step-child twice removed. All of which can bore men to tears. And then women ask men questions.

"Women ask men impossible to answer questions because the question we actually asked is not the question we really want answered. You only have to lie if you answer the question we actually asked rather than the one we really want answered. You would not have to lie if you ignored the question we actually asked and answered the question we really wanted answered. This is especially true if the question we actually asked requires the man to give

an opinion in his answer which is never permitted. (If a man gives a woman his opinion on any topic he should immediately apologize and humbly beg her forgiveness unless said opinion deals directly with automobiles or power tools.) Be advised that women ask these questions as a test. We are determining your ability to read subtext, deciding whether to continue the relationship or not, and seeing how clever you really are as shown by the quality of your answer. You will remember that women are naturally more sibylline than men and that we enjoy playing that delightful game "Confuse-A-Male". This has been a test. This has only been a test. If this had been an actual emergency requiring an opinion we would have asked a woman."

Think about that the next time you get deeply into the stats of your football league or begin discussing gear ratios on your latest automobile rebuild. If you smiled or laughed while reading the preceding quote, you are a man even I would like to meet. If not, your only defense is to use humor to save yourself. The more experienced man just ruefully shakes his head, grins, and admits that "hey he's male". Conceding the point in this way is very effective as it lets her win while reminding her of why you're both here.

If you are confused and seriously want her to explain what she means, ask her. If she likes you, she will explain.

Humor

If you can make her laugh, really laugh, you're usually in with a chance. We are not speaking of a polite titter here. If you do not get her reaching for a handkerchief or a napkin, it wasn't funny enough, try again. Be light, be kind, and be witty. By all means be exasperating if you have to go that far before she asks you to stop because laughing that much makes her ribs hurt.

You might run across a woman who gets the joke but will deliberately, and usually slyly, pretend to not get it.

You've met your match now, buddy. You're in for a round of two people deliberately and elaborately not getting each other's jokes. This game is called "Shot your Fox." The first person who actually breaks down and laughs, loses. With a sophisticated woman this can be fun and it is a good sign. A woman who is willing to play this game with you has already decided to bed you at the earliest opportunity unless you make a mistake.

Most mistakes that men make come more from saying too much rather than too little. There does come a point where it is best to just listen or to ask her dance, or ask if she's ready to go. If you're at a loss try "How about those Celtics?"

The point is to communicate with her by whatever means are necessary. You want her to receive your message clearly and you, usually, want a positive reaction from her.

Chemistry

It is there or it isn't. If she's wavering, there are some things you can do to tip the balance in your favor but if she's dead set against having anything to do with you there's nothing to be done. This has nothing to do with how you look, or with what you say or do. Here are three examples:

"He walked into the sports bar, horrible place, and joined the group, sitting down next to me. Everyone was talking and yet I could only think of how his hands and lips would feel on my skin. It didn't matter that he was not a young, hard-bodied, glamour male. I didn't care. It was all I could do to remain calm and not rip his clothes off and fuck him right then and there. I had to content myself with my leg against his but that was because we were so tightly packed together. Very crowded. Ah, but the goodnight kiss was so good—had to do it thrice!"

"He was suddenly drunk and hanging on the door so he didn't fall down. Didn't matter at all! He was tall with

dirty blond hair and buff from being used by his dad as a backhoe. He was chatting with the girl he was dating at the time but he managed to notice my roommate and me sitting there. Another guy wandered in and decided that I was the girl he wanted. I growled at him and flashed my fangs. He backed off saying oh my! But the drunken hunk loved it!"

"He was sitting at the bar. Nothing special about him particularly. Didn't matter. Oh how I wanted him! The thing was he was willing to accept and enjoy whatever I chose to offer him. We kissed and hugged several times, every time I went up for a drink. Circumstances meant nothing came of it but I will remember him to my grave."

As many professionals say, chemistry is the result of "positive vibrations" between two people. Obviously, there is some debate as to what exactly creates these vibrations, but most agree that attraction is amplified when we feel comfortable around someone. Negative vibrations arise from disagreements, overactive egos, competitiveness, and so on. Positive vibrations come about from being fun and exciting, conversing easily and effortlessly, and listening with an interest and a smile. Just sit across from her and act more comfortable than if you were at home in your plush recliner perhaps watching the Celtics.

Communicating Your Interest

You cannot just walk up to her and come on strong. You have to talk. More importantly you have to talk to her, specifically to her about her. This means you have to pay attention and notice things about her.

"Each woman is uniquely beautiful and worthy of being cherished. This thought is what separates the connoisseurs of women and the mere laymen. Every woman has that certain something that distinguishes her from everyone else. Picking out the details and acknowledging them, telling her, is what will set you apart in her mind.

Think about it: What did your girl wear last night? What did she say? Did you notice the tilt of her head, the mischief she held in her eyes or the way she bit her lip? Any time you feel that visceral tug, the urge to muss and take, tell her why and how you feel as you do. Recognize those triggers and let her know what she does to you.

Maybe you noticed how the sun lights up her hair, or the motion of her hand tucking a curl behind her ear. You could have been stirred by the sound of her laugh or maybe you stared transfixed at the lines of her body. She may have taken extra care getting ready for you, and her clothes, hair, and makeup are looking extra sharp. It could be the luscious curves in those hip-hugger jeans, or the soft sweater that clings to her curves—whatever it is that you're noticing, tell her about it."[7]

You will also note the advice extends to relationships with women beyond just the first few dates. She should not have to ask "Why are you still here?" You do not have to be a poet to say "You've got some beautiful legs there, baby girl" in a deeply appreciative tone of voice. Whatever it is, tell her about it. We do enjoy hearing from you.

Anatomy

I know you have studied this particular aspect of women very closely already so I will just cover two points every man must know.

1. The Grafenberg spot is an area on the front wall (toward the tummy) of the vagina, between the opening and the cervix, generally 2 to 3 inches inward from the opening. Theory dictates that the G-spot can be one of two things: either a bundle of nerves coming from the clitoris, or a gland (or series of glands) that produces lubrication, or both. Now, while all women own a spot with a G, not all of them find G-spot stimulation pleasurable. Just as with the

---

[7] askmen.com

clitoris, some women are more than eager, while others do not like it whatsoever. It is very sensitive. Only time will tell. Insert a finger (or two) into the vagina with your palm facing her mons pubis, that is to say towards her belly. Gently, bend your fingers frontward so that they lightly stroke the front wall of the vagina. Varying the degree of pressure also helps. She may ejaculate, yes we do it too, in which case, you have won the grand prize. No it isn't urine, it is a carbohydrate.

2. There are actually two types of multiple orgasms: sequential multiples and serial multiples. It can be difficult to tell the difference between the two—even for the woman. Distinguishing one type from the other is a matter of timing: Sequential multiple orgasms occur several minutes after one another, with an interruption in the arousal period in between, whereas serial multiples are separated only by seconds, producing one extended wave of pleasure. The latter is the truly rare form of the two. In some cases, orgasm can be difficult to achieve for she must be both relaxed and sexually aroused. All a man can do is his best. Try varying techniques slowly and savor the interlude.

Remember that sex improves upon further acquaintance as you learn her and she learns you and both of you relax around each other.

Techniques Every Man Must Know

1. Sexual multi-tasking. Doing two things at once. Which two is up to you.

2. Cunnilingus. Do it like you love it.

3. Body Worship. Think of it as Extreme Erotic Massage.

4. Caressing her G-Spot with the head of your penis. See what we meant when we said it is all in how you use it?

Alternative Play

It is up to you and the lady what you try, but there are 'best practices' even here.

Rule 1 is that both have to agree., willingly. If she declines to play, just let it go. You'll find someone else later.

MFM or FMF: More than two in the bed requires another decision. Who is to be bisexual or are the two of the same gender going to gang up on the third? Threesomes are fairly common. The spare person waits until play begins and then gently joins in.

Swinging

When a couple committed to each other mutually have sexual relationships with other persons for positive, life-enhancing, reasons. Several misconceptions concerning this topic linger in the minds of non-swingers.

1. Women are coerced or pressured into it.
2. Sex is sacred and swinging debases sex into simply a way to enjoy pleasure.

In the swing world, Women Rule. How ever they come to swing, once there, women find it liberating, confidence-building, and empowering. They can finally give up being 'nice girls'. They can stop worrying that they aren't 'cute' or 'pretty' enough. They can stop competing with other women and share instead. Women also find that men are not fiends and that often the best lovers are those they never expected. Women can opt in or opt out of any activity as they will and no questions are asked. They no longer have to justify their desires or their sexuality.

There is nothing wrong with pleasure, that is to say positive stimuli. The 'sacredness of sex' in all of this, lies within the relationship between the pair and not within the activity. Mistaking this key point leads non-swingers into error. Sharing joy and delight; enjoying your partner's having fun; learning about each other from watching their interactions with others—these are all good things. You grow both as individuals and as a couple. There is no fraud and no betrayal and you never need to feel as if there were. Everything is known. You have no secrets from each other. You may even learn something new about her along the way and she of you. But if you cannot walk up to another man and say "My lady would like you to have her number" you do not belong here.

BDSM

Here you have to be careful because you can truly harm yourselves. Be advised that contrary to popular belief, the submissive holds the power while the dominant has sole responsibility for whatever happens. At a word from the submissive, all play immediately stops and the submissive is released. Without delay. No questions asked.

"His sexual subjugation should be joyous and life affirming. This somewhat less than silken dalliance should be fun for both with each one pleasing the other. This result cannot be achieved without mutual regard and respect. There also has to be a mutual sexual attraction. If the blood is not roaring within, then nothing good can come of playing in this fashion. In many ways, the actual acts are the same and only the perspective changes. Fellatio becomes feeding off the male, for example, when done from a female superior position. The male takes on the passive role during sex unless called upon to please his lady. While there are no set rules, play should be mutually satisfying with both having orgasms. There are men who can wear a collar and leash with a great deal of panache. I have seen this. He was wearing only a 'bad boy' grin and sitting on my sofa at the time."

You may only restrain another person for 45 minutes at any one time and you must never, ever leave a restrained person alone. This is serious stuff and great care must be taken to ensure that no harm comes of it. One of you should have a decent amount of experience before introducing another to this variety of sexual play.

As long as you both enjoy it, and no harm comes from it, few things are completely out of bounds. I only ask that you be responsible and sensible adults about this.

Relationships

Scary word to most men but it needn't be for relationships can take many forms. The only rule here is to be up front about what you want and to take her desires seriously. If she wants an exclusive relationship and you do not, then she is not the woman for you.

"Relationships, even the freedom-oriented ones, are based on give-and-take and a solid sense of equality. So if you're planning to date several men at once, don't get all bent out of shape when he dates several women; by playing the field, you're giving him the license to do the same. In fact, it may be in your best interest to actually encourage such behavior... provided it's subtle. You're equals in everything, and if you're going to play around, so can he. It's simply a matter of keeping everything pointed in the right direction." [8]

In modern parlance you will hear of 'fuckbuddies', FWB, STR, LTR, and NSA. Each of these have a precise definition. Fuckbuddies are people who repeatedly have sex with each other with no emotions at all. It is just sex and then get the hell out. FWB stands for friends with benefits where you two actually like each other and enjoy each other's company both in and out of the bed. STR is short term relationship, generally for just the summer as an example. LTR is long term relationship which will last for as long as it lasts, there is no set time limit. NSA is no strings attached. Meaning no commitments of any kind—

---

[8] askmen.com

no kids, no diseases and no falling in love, thank you very much.

Men wear condoms. Get used to it. Women take care of birth control. Be aware that some women are allergic to latex but there are non-latex condoms out there. Some women are allergic to the coatings on condoms and not the latex itself. Some experimentation may be necessary, on her part, to find this out. Ask her if you have questions. Some women cannot handle The Pill which is the most reliable form of birth control other than not having sex at all. There are other methods available. If she is proposing to have sex with you, her status in this regard becomes your business. Any health issues either of you have becomes your partner's business once sex becomes involved. Speak up. Remember that while sex is great, it isn't worth dying for. If you are sexually active with multiple partners get yourself tested regularly.

Demand equality and reciprocity from women. If she wants to sport date and play the field, you are to have the same privileges. If she wants you to spend hours petting her, then she should be willing to pet you in return for hours. Do not let her get away with being 'selfish' in your relationships. Doing so will only erode her respect for you and bring the relationship to an early end.

Within relationships, communication between partners becomes increasingly important over time. Relationships will change and some emotional attachment might happen. Expect to have to re-negotiate the terms of your relationship as it goes along. One item is of crucial importance, there are to be no 'silent treatments' and no tantrums. If you cannot speak of it like an adult, then it is either not important or you are too close to the problem. Back off and discuss it later. Yelling at each other will only make the problem worse. Forget 'making up'—just a waste of time as it only glosses over the issue—it doesn't address it and it doesn't solve it.

It is also important for each of you to remain their own person. This means that they retain their own opinions and their own identities. If a common household is not contemplated then expect to spend time apart. Going out with your posse' is expected, and she can go out with hers. As long as the relationship remains fair and equal, there should be few problems maintaining it. Consult frequently even if it is just to coordinate your schedules.

Polyamory

Now you're an acknowledged couple and yet, she has other men friends and you have other girlfriends. You are a pair of polyamorists. Polyamory is a network of emotional attachments of varying degrees of intimacy. This can get complicated. Consider her schedule if she has work, kids, and several men as her secondaries in addition to a husband acting as her primary relationship. Then add in your wife and your other secondary, in addition to the previous lady, your kids, and your work. There's also her husband's work and your wife's work, and all of the kids have to be driven to their after school activities. Heaven help you if someone gets ill! Then your relatives want to come and visit and so do hers. Not only do you need a program to keep track of who is who but you need differential calculus to work out the timing of who does what when and with whom. These intertwined relationships work as long as everyone trusts the strength of their bonds, obeys the ground rules, and behaves as an adult.

And here you thought just maintaining a relationship with only one woman was difficult.

A sense of humor, willingness to see the other side, and generosity of spirit are what is needed to keep a relationship going. Effective communication outside of the bedroom is the key. Granted, you may gotten hold of the wrong woman, in which case there's nothing you can do but sever the relationship. But is she is still Ms. Right, treat her as you want her to treat you and gently call her on it when she doesn't. If you say you will do it, do it— whatever it might be—and get it done. Lend her a hand now and again. Have her lend you a hand every once in a while. She can read the instruction manual while you try to change framostat or the muffler bearings, or whatever. Just set out a comfy chair in the garage, make sure she has her drinks, cigarettes, lighter, and ashtray, and hand her the book. Do it together.

Both of you do have to be honest and tell the truth. This does not give either of you license to be brutal, you both can employ some tact. But if she cannot accept the truth of who you are and what you want or are willing to give then she's not the lady for you and vice versa. If there is no trust and understanding between you two, then there's no relationship.

The End

Breaking up is hard—there's no doubt. The longer the relationship, the harder the breaking up will be. Generally speaking it takes two years to 'get over' a past relationship whether it is divorce, death or just 'mutual incompatibility'. Now, gentlemen do not talk. They also don't whine.

All parties have to there in person. Face to face is the only way. Be gentle but firm and implacable. No backing away from the issue. No chasing after her. Why try to be with someone who doesn't want you? Move out and move on. Then say nothing. He said/she said fights do nothing but send you off into a downward spiral of tit for tat recriminations which is worthless. The same rules apply regardless of who kicked who out.

If it is divorce, get a good divorce lawyer and make him/her work for their pay. If you have kids, don't make them pay—you're still their dad and they'll miss you. Besides, it might irritate her to know how great a dad you are.

Afterwards, get your life back in order before trying to date again. Women can smell desperation a mile away. Focus on work, your kids, your buddies, your hobbies, anything but 'The Chase'. When it is time, go back to the section on older men and try this 'dating thing' again. Good luck!

That being said....

Do not get lax during your relationships. Taking her for granted, being difficult to live with, always being argumentative, not finishing what you start, and generally being a pain will kill any relationship. Learn to effectively communicate and keep on communicating. Having a home with a loving partner as your 'safe haven' is not so terrible after all.

Love as you live – unstintingly!

Common Myths

1. **Women do not like sex**. Entirely false. Every woman has her own appetite, of course but usually one self-aware woman can out-gun any six men you'd care to name. Just as stress, ill health, over work, and so on affect men so too do they affect women.

2. **Women are prone to mood swings**. Perhaps, but if they tend to be all that wild, it may not be just the normal hormonal stress. Medical assistance maybe required. In any case, no one should have to put up with this. Be even tempered and demand the same from her.

3. **Women are emotional.** Sure and so are you but we are permitted to show our emotions, to a point. You have to decide what level of emotion suits you and deal with the issue from there.

4. **Women are irrational**. Also entirely false. We just see it differently than you do. From our point of view, you just don't understand. Effective communication is the key.

5. **Women cannot make up their minds**. Sometimes but then again you have the same problem from time to time. Some people are just more decisive than others.

6. **Women always change their minds**. Not always. As the situation changes so might the decisions. This is more situational than sexual.

7. **Women are unreliable**. Most women are doing three things, at least, at once. Multi-tasking isn't easy. If it were, men would be doing it.

Generally if the sentence begins with "women are..." you can discount it. Some women might be whatever and some aren't. Every person is a mix of delights and irritations.

This book may seem far too slender to you. You may feel that 'it isn't enough' but I assure you that it is. Under all that glamour and allure beats a human heart. Reach that and she'll reach for you as often as you will reach for her.

Conclusion

My reason for writing this book is my being tired of watching men self-destruct when it comes to women. I have a great deal of sympathy for men but, really, the elementary mistakes you fellows make are enough to make one weep. Disrespect, insults, taunts—they get you nowhere. Stop trying to get noticed by doing the wrong things. Stop being metro-sexual. Be neat, clean, presentable and yet male to the core. Go to where the type of woman you want hangs out, mingle, talk to women without immediate expectations, get her name and number, avoid making promises, do not suck up to her—just relax. If she wants you, she will let you know.

If you don't go, you won't get.

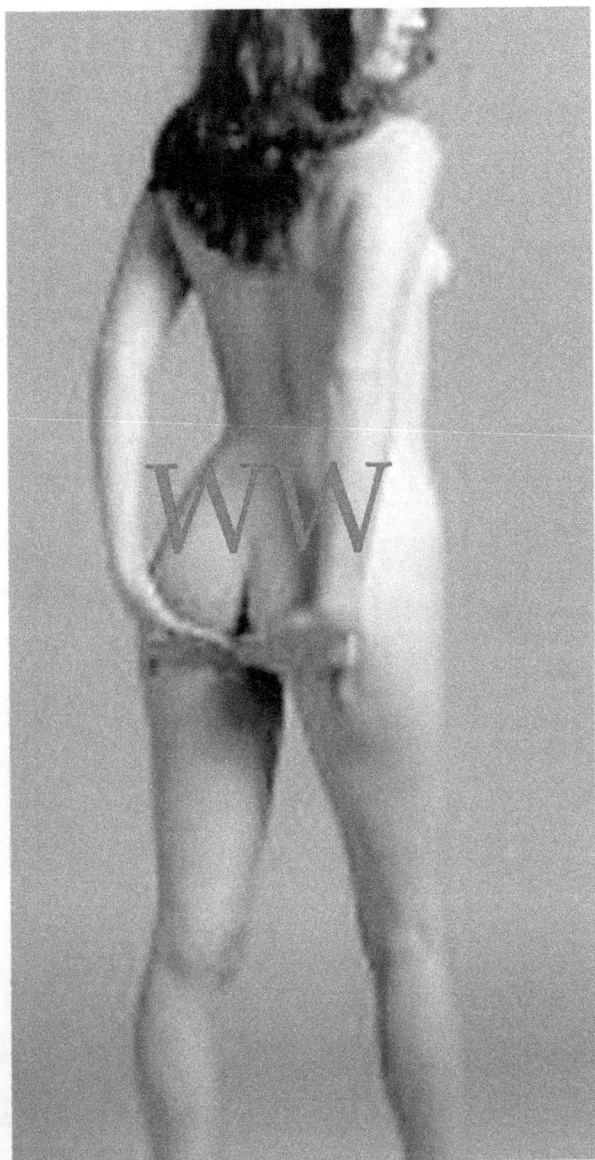

by Corbis

Wicked Woman Day Spa for Men

WW

The Wicked Woman Day Spa for Men provides every customer with care, with concern, and with services specifically designed to meet the needs of the tired, careworn, work-a-day male.

Our highly trained staff of Delightful Demonesses will help you look and feel you're best so you can face your day with confidence and ease.

We offer both at-home care and services at our spa facility. No matter which location suits your needs, you will receive the best of care.

Appointments are available on a first come, first served basis from 9am to 3pm and from 7pm to 12 midnight, Monday through Thursday.

Call reception for your appointment today!

WW Spa Service Packages
Package 1

1. A nice romp in the bed; 2. shave; 3. facial mask using volcanic mud; 4. hair trimming—various areas; 5. shoulder massage with scented oil; 6. hot shower being vigorous scrubbed down using scented body wash—everywhere; 7. dried with warm towels; 8. anointed with scented oils—select areas; 9. fellatio; 10. wrapped in a warm robe and given a scotch and a cigarette and laid on a sofa and fed grapes.

Package 2

1. A delightful romp with one of our demonesses; 2. a brief rest break in a darkened room; 3. a full massage back and front specially designed for male bodies; 4. Fellatio; 5. a salt scrub in the shower with extra warm water rinsing depending upon degree of furriness; 6. Skin care treatment; 7. Manicure and a glass of single-malt scotch with an ice cube while wearing a warm spa robe.

These packages are recommended thrice weekly.

Package 3

1. An extended romp with two Demonesses; 2. Hair trimming and a shave and manicure simultaneously; 3. Full body massage by all three Demonesses with scented body oils; 4. Volcanic mud facial; 5. Sea salt scrub and scented body wash with warm water rinsing; 6. Dried with warmed towels; 7. Fellatio from the third Demoness; 8. skin care treatment; 9. Relaxing on the sofa in a darkened room with a scotch, a cigar and soothing music.

This package is recommended as a monthly treatment for especially stressed teddybears.

When calling for an appointment, please specify which package you require and whether you want us to come to you or if you will be coming to us.

Please note that this is NOT a serious offering of spa or of sexual services.
The intent is to amuse and delight only.

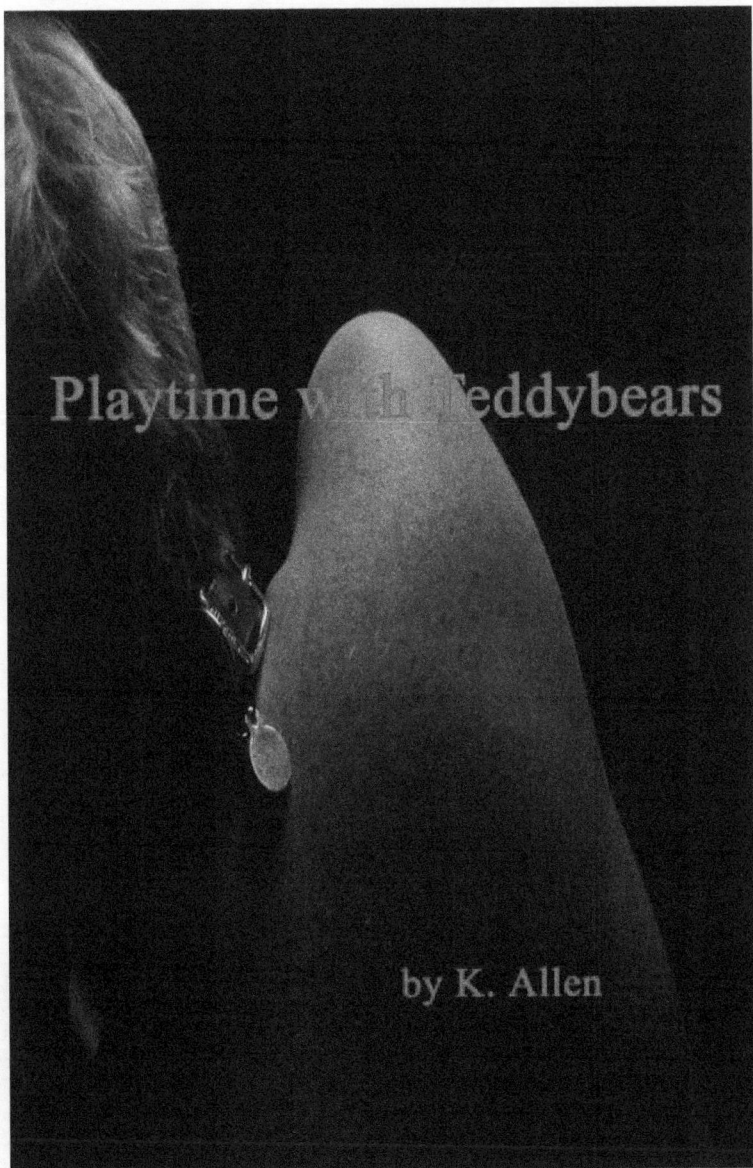

Playtime with Teddybears

by K. Allen

by K. Zupan

**Dedicated to
James Eck
and
Teddybears
everywhere**

"know that you are loved"

Rewards

Back beneath his collar and kneeling at the end of his bed, fondling and kissing my breasts while sliding his hands up and along my legs and thighs and periodically wrapping one arm around me he then moved on down, kissing my body until he began cunnilingus while still caressing me. Several orgasms late, mmmmm I love orgasms, I gently pulled on his collar and put my crossed ankles onto his left shoulder as he entered me. Oh yes, right there. Yes, Just like that. My back arches and I lightly run my claws down the front of his thighs as he moves inside of me. He then began climbing onto the bed, one knee, then the other as I wrapped my legs around him. He came, as I did, when I gently bit his shoulder. I love hearing him cum. But I don't' let him stop there. I squeeze him and continue to move, doubling him. Now it is time for his massage. I begin on his back. This is a real massage suited to the heavier musculature of men. I put my full weight into it, working his flesh into submission. As his body relaxes shoulders and wrists down through his legs, I begin gently drawing arabesques onto his skin with my claws, kissing, him, licking his skin, touching him with my lips, hair, and body; sliding up and down along his length. Kissing the nape of his neck I whisper that it is time for him to roll over. He does and I begin again with my heavy handed techniques then move up and begin gently licking the corner of his eye with the tip of my tongue, then over his lips and kissing at the point of his jaw moving from side to side, then down his throat, his chest, his stomach. Then I breathe onto his cock without touching him. Slowly, ever so very slowly, I take him into my mouth. And begin attempting to remove his brains from his skull via his penis. Resistance is futile. Men are so cute when they cannot move afterwards and when they regain movement they tend to walk sideways which is also cute. Please don't fall down. You're too big for me to lift. Snuggling on the sofa until

212

he's gotten his breath back. I lie diagonally onto his bed and he scoops me up into his arms, kisses, mmmmm, and then I slide him in oh yes, more, more, and more. Without missing a move we go into scissors and then his reward. I slyly move his cock out and back a bit and we're spooning but at a 90 degree angle and I slide him up into my ass. Moving together he soon orgasmed and we lay there with him still inside for several minutes. Mmmmm, you're welcome, baby.

See you tomorrow.

Uncollared

Lying on his bed in the candlelight wrapped in each other's arms and lips. What began languidly became a torrid, wild banshee fuck where each orgasm led to six more as an uncollared teddybear displayed his aggressive nature. What big strong arms you have, baby! He deployed all his 'arts', and earned a few claw marks, but the demands of the day made this first round quicker than most. One thing always leads to another with me and the sight of a naked teddybear lying face- up on his bed is more than I can ignore. Pouncing upon him, I nuzzle down his body then up his thighs—very slowly. Caressing his body with my hair, a breast, a leg, lips and hands; all flowing and wrapping around him as I move lower and get into position. I gently breathed along the length of his cock and took up the head in my mouth without closing my lips upon it; just lightly flickering the tip of the head with my tongue. Then I swallowed him whole in one motion, closed my lips and wrapped my throat around him and came up with a twisting movement. Up hard and strong with a twist while also pressing my tongue against the base of his penis as if trying to bend it backwards; down gently and soft—repeatedly. Wheee! Up on top and moving and getting him all soaking wet as I cum again and again until straddling him and hugging him fiercely, he too orgasms. This break I spend it wandering around sideways while he chuckles and tries to not walk sideways himself while steering me to the sofa. La la la, giggle. Naked teddybears should never lie down on their beds when I'm in the vicinity. Even if they are lying face-down. I laid on top of him and began nibbling on his ears and breathing on the side of his neck. Then as he brought his shoulders up, I bent his head down slightly and passionately, firmly, kissed the nape of his neck. His responsive quiver shook his entire body. I slid around him, while 'feathering' him and we ended up with me on my back at the edge of the bed with him standing there, my legs (ankles crossed) over his one shoulder, having more orgasms. This time he didn't make it to the sofa but sat on the floor with his head back so I could kiss him some more.

Office Visit

Your hands on my skin, massaging and caressing, such nice strong hands—purrrrr. So nice to have you come by. Warm up with some coitus. Oh my! It has been awhile so you came rather quickly. We shall have to do more of this. A small break and then lie down, sweety, and let the evil kitten have her way with you. I think I may have left a few marks this time. I love riding you! Oh yeah! I cum all over you and get you all wet. This time I am not holding back anything. You get it all this time. There's the desk. Shall we try that? Yes! Now it is your turn to cum. Wow!! You have to stop by my office more often! A naked man in your office makes work much more delightful!

Dreamtime

Ah! I am the most fortunate of evil kittens! Not only was he eager for my attention but he also displayed a deep appreciation for me. We began with body worship. He is truly a most gifted lover! Tonight was a slow and most intimate adventure. Then he was in me. Very, very nice! Felt so good. Several orgasms later, we moved to the end of the bed and I leaned over it with him behind and in me. Also very good! I ran my claws gently up the backs of his legs and he learned another thing about himself. Tracing thin lines with the edges of my claw-tips makes him quiver with ecstasy. We both enjoyed an orgasm and then, laughing with sheer joy, I fell onto the bed, rolled over and he began cunnilingus. Oh my! With mouth and hand he brought me to more orgasms! Wonderful! His turn came next as I straddled him and came repeatedly all over him. He loves the sensations, sights and sounds of a wild tumultuous kitten enjoying herself. Then we enjoyed the most intimate of activities—we curled up together and napped. There is no greater indication of trust than when a woman naps within the comfort of your arms. I stirred and then was petted awake for more fun and then we returned to napping. So sweet. He is tremendous fun!

It Begins

I had a certain 'agenda' in mind for him tonight. I shall experiment with him over the course of our encounter. We will move from the familiar to the new gradually so as to not make him uncomfortable. Naked, there in the candlelight with music playing, first we cuddled and then coitus with him up. Then I tied him down onto the bed with the straps and cuffs. Kneeling on the bed between his spread legs, hiding the vibe between my thighs, I began doing body worship moving from his face downward with excruciating slowness. Exploring him and his sensitivity. Slowly, slowly, slowly kissing here, lightly licking there, a little nibbling, little nuzzling—mmmmm fur. Sliding by, I moved to the ankles and ran slowly up each leg, one at a time. Easing up to his scrotum, taking first the one side, then the other sucking and licking while I activated the vibe which I then gently placed beneath his scrotum onto the peritoneum, I then began fellatio with the vibe held against him with just the right amount of movement and pressure. Up and down and twisting and licking and sucking both upward as well as downward and with the vibe having its stimulating effect- he didn't last very long. I released him and was engulfed in a huge bear hug which ended up with me sitting astride him and riding him vigorously. He and the bed got very wet. This lasted for some time as the sight of a woman thoroughly enjoying herself stimulates him. He never wants me to hold back. He begs for my full, for all of my sexual responses. I have not yet given those to him. Soon, very soon now he will receive them.

Teddybear's Lap Dance

I wore black leather gloves, black leather wristbands with silver spikes, my black leather and silver chain outfit and black stilettos.

My tunes were "Evil Angel" by Rufus Wainwright, "Clubbed2Death (Kurayamino Mix)" by Rob D and "Lucky You" by the Deftones.

Sitting in the chair in the center of his living room rug, music begins and I slink about oozing around him in a slow circle getting closer and closer, sneaking up on him in time to the slinky music. When the song ended I was behind him and covered his eyes with my gloved hands until the next song came on. This song's a real hip-swinging tune so I was moving and undulating up close and personal, straddling his legs, undoing his shirt buttons, breathing on the side of his neck, in and out, and around and back but with energy and fired with dark purpose. Then back to covering his eyes for the next song, back to slinky again. This time I gently trailed the spikes along his arms and thighs as well as stalking him in a feline manner. He was very stoic and didn't move an inch, something else did, but then he wasn't sweating so I must need more practice.

Teddybear Testride

It began sitting side by side on the sofa with him naked. We progressed slowly since he was nervous, not knowing what to expect. *EG* But I laid the training collar out onto the coffee table and let him play with it a bit while I played with him. Then I stood up, faced him and slowly removed my sweater, my pants, and then my bra. (I love that little gasp men make when they see me naked.) I straddled him, facing him, while he sat on the sofa and placed the collar around his neck and asked him what he wanted to do. He opted to suck my nipples, so I led him to the bed, sat on the edge of it, and said yes. Hmmm he was very good. I then removed my underwear (beige lace boy shorts) and he slowly licked down my body and began cunnilingus. Ahhh! So nice! I then took his right hand (wrong hand) and he switched to his left and began G-Spot caressing. OMG! The first of many orgasms and he got very wet. I squirt. He seemed to like it from what he seemed to say at the time. We then played find my birthmarks (I have two; one on each side). He didn't have his glasses on so he had to examine my skin very closely to find them. I love being nuzzled like that. There I was purrrring and he was doing his very best to stimulate every inch of me. Licking, kissing, nuzzling, caressing. Mmmmmmmmmmmmmeow. It was getting too warm for him so while I put on his condom, he removed the collar. We then slide in and out—he was curved just right. The head of his penis rubbing right there! Oh wow! That was good! then, in the interest of checking off all the boxes on my checklist, we went to doggy style and he came—very loud, very hard. It was terrific! I hugged him until he stopped shaking, kissed him, and then we took a break. During the break he put on the collar and began caressing me until I took him back to the bed and had him lie down. I then pounced upon him and began exploring him, finding out all of his special places with hands, lips, and tongue. A bit of fellatio and he was more than ready for the next condom (I put on all condoms btw). Then I was up on top of him, thoroughly enjoying myself to the point where I flushed bright pink and ejaculated all over him! He kept saying things—I am not sure just what but he seemed to be enjoying the sight of my enjoying him. Aaaah! Such a lovely man! The collar had had to come off again. Too hot when he's active. Then I rolled off of him, laughing, and he decided to return the favor and pounced upon me. Meow! Some more in and out and I came, he came, we all came. More hugs and then I teased him with the idea of tasting his semen. EG He grinned but said eeeeek! I laughed and said too early, huh? He grinned back, he had gotten over being nervous by his time, and agreed, too early. We snuggled up together on the sofa, drank some more (soda) and then went off to shower together. Well, I showered first since I like it much hotter than he does. A warm towel later and he decided to invite me back to his place and some pinot noir next week for some further fun and Teddybear Education since he said he would like to become one of my male Sluts.

I was a very happy Kitten having had so many orgasms and he felt both drained and relaxed. Think he passed his 'testride'?

Seduced Into Sexual Subjugation

He had no idea how absolutely mind-blowing his sexual subjugation would be. But he trusted me. I began by having him disrobe then collaring him and placing cuffs around his wrists. I then attached his wrist cuffs to the tethering strap at the head of his bed. I became naked, straddled his body, kissed him then slowly kissed the corner of one eye, nuzzled slowly down his cheek to his ear and then ran the tip of my tongue lightly along his jaw and then over his lips—very, very gently. I kissed the corner of his other eye and nibbled on his ear lobe and licked lightly up the edge of his ear then down to his neck. I kissed his throat beneath his chin then slowly with hands, tongue and body caressed my way further south, tracing gentle arabesques with my claws and fingertips—sometimes ghosting over the tips of his fur, other times using the edges of my claws to tantalize his skin. My breath slid over his skin where I had moistened it causing his nipples to harden. Settling down between his thighs I ran my hands lightly up his legs while gently breathing on, without touching, his cock—his breath caught in his throat. I took his testicles one at a time into my mouth and sucked and licked, flickering with my tongue. He was moaning very softly. Then I swallowed him and loosely, gradually closing my mouth around his cock without pressure. Slowly I increased the pressure and began sliding up and down and around his cock. Teasing the head with my tongue as I sucked and rotated around his cock. Just enough to make him extremely willing and compliant. I rose up and slid him inside of me and began using him for my enjoyment. Up and forward then down and back, faster and faster. Ah! So very nice! I remember that I was smiling. then sitting back on him and scrubbing back and forth rapidly. Repeating the pattern as I had orgasm after orgasm juicing all over him all the while. OMG! was, I think, what he said when he orgasmed. He was still quivering when he tried to follow me to the sofa for a break afterwards. He almost had a double orgasm that night. We'll work on that!

Stroking The Bones

Hmmm come and pet me, baby, with those long light touches you do so well all up and down my body, one hand caressing the front of my hip, the other hand stroking the back of my leg as your lips kiss and nuzzle just beneath one buttock until your hand finds my G-Spot and your tongue finds my peritoneum. Oh yeah! Feels so very good! Then it is quickly into our favorite position of you standing at the edge of the bed with me on my back and my crossed ankles onto your shoulder with you deeply inside being squeezed as you move in and out. I love hearing you cum as much as you love hearing me. Now that the preliminaries are over, I have two new things for you to try. You kneel on the bed staying upright, your back to me and with greased hands I begin caressing you while pressing my lips on the back of your neck, nibbling your ears, and breathing on the sides of your neck as my hands slowly and firmly slide all over your body. Accept the pleasure you feel. Enjoy it; suspending all thought. One hand sliding down the front of your throat while the other caresses your testicles from behind. Then up your spine while caressing your penis. Always three points of contact for while my hands are busy so to is my mouth or my body sliding along your skin. Slowly. Repeatedly. Building but never enough to bring you to orgasm. Lie down onto your back. I begin fellatio then bring the vibe up underneath and behind your scrotum slowly moving it down and back until I find your G-Spot with it. How you love it! Your penis deep in my throat, my hand holding your testicles and that vibe gently moving just so. But your orgasm is mine to control and you are not permitted to move. Accept the pleasure you feel. Let it run freely through you. Up, down, in, out, twisting, hard, soft, gentle, and rough—over and over again. Leaving the vibe where it is, I sit on top of you and take you inside me. Now. Yes, now! A short wild ride as I cum all over you and you cum inside of me. Yes!! I get up and pull on your legs, stretching you a bit as you relax. Feels so good. I tidy up leaving you time to recover from your first male G-Spot orgasm. Deep slow breaths, baby, there's more to come. Now we're going to enjoy sex with strength. It is my own original technique called stroking the bones. There's nothing light and tantalizing here. Now it is just controlled masculine strength and ardor as you with heavy hands ignore the usual erogenous zones and instead focus on the bones in my body. Sliding down the arms, across the shoulders, along the ribs, around the shoulder blades. Your greased hands holding and moving me as you exerting all of your strength. Then the spine from the back of the skull slowly down all of the way to my coccyx. Oh that feels so overwhelming! Again and again! Aah!! Then the pelvis and the down the legs. I had been kneeling at the edge of the bed, now I rotate to face you as you kneel there and wrap myself around you—totally ignited. On hand firmly holding me to you as your mouth seeks my breast and your other hand finds my G-Spot again. Then I am kissing you violently while clawing your back and rump. Biting your shoulders. Highly erotic wild power sex as I rotate again and stand before you bent over and you enter inside. Yes, now! Go! WOW!

Never fear to cut loose, sweety. I will not break.

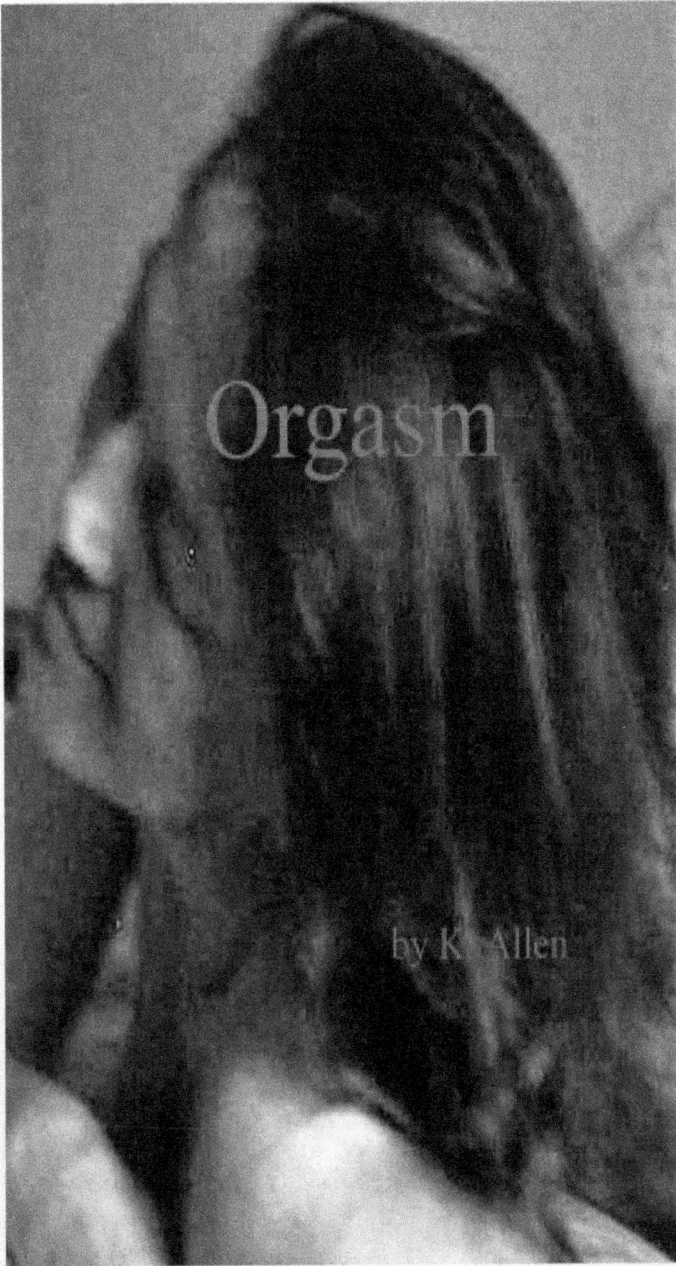

Orgasm

by K. Allen

by James Eck

for all of you

Contents

Definition

The peak of sexual arousal, when all the muscles that were tightened during sex relax. This causes a pleasurable feeling that involves the genital area and sometimes the entire body. Muscles throughout the body spasm, including those of the pelvic floor, anus, vagina and uterus. During orgasm, most people experience increased heartbeat rates, faster breathing, dilation of the pupils, and increased blood pressure. The increase in blood pressure can result in flushing and the skin feeling hot to the touch. Endorphins are released into the bloodstream causing feelings of pleasure, joy, giddiness, warmth, sleepiness or excitement.

After orgasm, humans often feel tired and a need to rest. This was recently attributed to the release of prolactin. Prolactin is a typical neuroendocrine response in depressed mood and irritation. Ongoing research at the University Medical Center of Groningen, the Netherlands, studies brain events that accompany orgasm in men and women. Techniques used involve Positron Emission Tomography (PET) and fMRI. Male and female brains act almost the same during orgasm. Brain scans showed that large parts of the cerebral cortex temporarily reduced their activity.

There are several physiological components of orgasm. First, orgasm is a total body response, not just a pelvic event. Brain wave patterns have shown distinct changes during orgasm, and muscles in many different areas of the body contract during this phase of sexual response. Some people experience the involuntary contraction of facial muscles resulting in what looks like a grimace or an expression of discomfort or displeasure, but it is actually an indication of high sexual arousal.

The most characteristic physical feature of orgasm is the sensation produced by the simultaneous rhythmic contractions of the pubococcygeus muscle (pc muscle). Along with contractions of the anal sphincter, rectum and perineum, the uterus and outer third of the vagina (the orgasmic platform) for women, and the ejaculatory ducts and muscles around the penis for men, this constitutes the reflex of orgasm.

The first few contractions are intense and close together, occurring at about 0.8-second intervals. As orgasm continues, the contractions diminish in intensity and duration and occur at less frequent intervals Despite the anatomical differences between male and female genitals, orgasms in men and women are physiologically and psychologically, or subjectively, very similar.

Sexual Response Cycle

Each person has a unique sexual response cycle, and any discussion of the abstract "human" sexual response necessarily must gloss over these differences. Sexual response is an extremely individualistic experience.

These stages in the sexual response cycle are not limited to traditional sexual intercourse. These steps describe reactions to masturbation, oral sex, fantasy, etc. Remember this when embarking on your exploration of your own sexual response cycle.

This list should not be used as a checklist when observing your own sexual responses. If one tries to act as an observer during sexual experiences, one will likely become a spectator – as if watching one's self engaging in sexual acts, noting and commenting on the events. This greatly detracts from your own and your partner's enjoyment of sex. Try to prevent this tendency in yourself.

Masters and Johnson: The Sexual Response Cycle

Pioneering sex researchers Masters and Johnson broke the human sexual response cycle down into these phases. A discussion of each individual step follows.

- Excitement
- Plateau
- Orgasm
- Resolution
- Refractory Period

Sexologist Helen Singer Kaplan has developed an alternate vision of the sexual response cycle, which includes "Desire" as the first item on the list. Since not all sexual activity is prefaced by desire, we consider the traditional Masters and Johnson description to be more accurate.

Excitement

This is the first phase in the sexual response cycle. As with all later stages, excitement varies in duration and intensity from person to person and even from sexual encounter to sexual encounter. This phase can last anywhere from a few minutes to several hours.

Vasocongestion and myotonia, two basic physiological mechanisms, affect both men and women during this and subsequent phases.

Vasocongestion is the filling up with blood and subsequent swelling of body tissues. Thus, the penis becomes erect in a man and in a woman the breasts, labia, nipples and clitoris swell. A sexual flush can occur on the cheeks.

Myotonia is the increased muscular tension that occurs during arousal. Some of these muscular reactions are voluntary while others are involuntary. The most obvious examples are the muscular contractions that accompany both male and female orgasms.

The penis may become fully or partially erect. The testes engorge with blood and move upward. In women, the clitoral shaft enlarges while the inner and outer labia separate and enlarge. Most women also produce vaginal lubrication at this stage.

Plateau

In this stage, sexual excitement increases to orgasm. This phase can be very brief, from a couple of seconds to few minutes. Most people experience more intense orgasms when this phase of sexual response is lengthened.

All the physiological reactions mentioned above intensify. Heartbeat and breathing rate accelerate, muscle tension rises, and sexual flushes are more noticeable. The outer third of the vagina engorges with blood.

Despite the title, this plateau is not a static and boring place. The Masters and Johnson plateau is a thrilling spiral toward orgasm.

Orgasm

This stage lasts only a few seconds – the shortest in the sexual response cycle. Women usually have a longer-lasting orgasm than men.

For men, seminal fluids gather in the ejaculatory ducts and urethra. This produces a feeling of inevitability about the orgasm. Then the semen is ejaculated at the time of orgasm. Note that orgasm and ejaculation are two separate physiological processes in men, although they almost always occur simultaneously.

For women, the uterus and vagina contract in rhythmic waves.

Interestingly enough, the feelings of orgasm do not seem to vary between the genders. Several studies in which men and women are asked to describe their feelings during orgasm have shown that reports cannot be classified by gender. Men and women alike tend to describe orgasm with phrases like "waves of pleasure in my body," which seems to describe the rhythmic muscular contractions that occur.

Resolution

During this phase, the body slowly returns to its original, unexcited state. The resolution phase begins immediately after orgasm unless stimulation continues. Some of the effects of sexual excitement last longer than others.

Refractory Period

For men, the refractory period is the time during which they cannot reach excitement, plateau or orgasm through any type of stimulation. The duration of this period varies greatly, from a few minutes to a day or two.

Women do not experience this period in the sexual response cycle. Women are capable of achieving orgasm at any time during resolution – although many women don't find orgasms beyond the first to be as pleasurable. Women are truly capable of multiple orgasms because of this lack of a refractory period.

Please keep in mind that these stages of sexual response are as individual as human beings. There is no right or wrong way to experience the sexual response cycle. Instead, focus on exploring your own and learning more about your body and your personal sexual response.

Female Orgasm

Although some researchers believe there is only one type of female orgasm, others report that different types of stimulation can cause two different types of orgasms. The different female orgasm types can create totally different sensations for different women.

Inside the vagina, on the ventral side of the vaginal wall, there's a particularly sensitive spot called the G spot (short for Grafenberg spot, after the scientist who first observed this phenomenon). Stimulation of the G spot can create a particularly intense form of female orgasm.

Most women need a break after a female orgasm, to stop or greatly reduce sex play, because they feel too sensitive to enjoy continued stimulation. After a rest, they may or may not be ready to experience more orgasms. But some women don't need to stop after a single orgasm, and can have several in a row. This phenomenon is called experiencing multiple orgasms and isn't uncommon.

Some women and couples perceive achieving female orgasm as the most important element of sexual intercourse. This is not the case – so long as you both enjoy yourselves, there is no reason to overemphasize female orgasm. If you do not experience orgasm at all during sex play, these guidelines will help you and your partner achieve female orgasm.

Women who know how to achieve female orgasm are generally women who masturbate. They know what kinds of stimulation they like and where they like it. They are more likely to have examined their own genitalia and are less inhibited about their bodies, less embarrassed by them.

To orgasm, a woman has to give herself permission to enjoy sex; to embrace and accept her sexuality. She must be relaxed yet aroused and open to pleasure. Achieving this state can be difficult for some women. In order to create the optimal environment for achieving female orgasm, you and your partner should engage in foreplay until you are excited and ready for intercourse. Achieving female orgasm is not like running a race. There is no goal – only the process, the experience, of stimulation. Many women start thinking of an orgasm as the finish line of their personal race when instead they should pay attention to the path they are running. Focus on feeling pleasure.

The mysteries of the female orgasm are not so much in what physiological effects they cause, but rather how to experience more and better orgasms. The more a woman knows about her own body, and about female orgasms and orgasm techniques in general, the more likely she will be to have orgasms when alone and when with her partner or partners.

Vaginal orgasms

A vaginal orgasm is relatively uncommon due to the relative lack of sensitive nerve endings that can be easily stimulated in and around the vagina. The most sensitive parts of the vagina are at the opening and within the first two inches of the opening. Some women also find that beneath the cervix and farther back into the vagina, there is another sensitive spot capable of inducing orgasms.

During a vaginal orgasm, the uterus drops lower, shortening the vagina. Presumably this shortens the distance that sperm must travel to fertilize the female egg.

The term "vaginal orgasm" has created a great degree of confusion since Sigmund Freud told the world that mature women only experience orgasm when their vaginas, rather than their clitorises, were stimulated. This placed a great deal of importance on the man's penis – exactly where most men think it should be. This is utter nonsense. Vaginal orgasms are no more or less mature than clitoral orgasms – simply different.

Clitoral orgasms

The clitoris has more nerve endings in its tiny tip than the entire glans (head) of a man's penis. For this reason, most women experience orgasms far more easily during clitoral stimulation. Most women masturbate by stimulating the clitoris.

During a clitoral orgasm, the vagina actually becomes longer, creating a pocket to be formed under the uterus. Many women like a feeling of fullness, provided by a penis, dildo or fingers, while experiencing a clitoral orgasm.

Blended orgasms

A third type of orgasm is experienced when both vaginal and clitoral stimulation occur simultaneously. This is described as more intense and sometimes known as a "full-body" orgasm, because the escalation and release of muscular tension affects the entire body.

G-Spot orgasms

The term "G-Spot" was first introduced to the public at large in the book, "The G Spot and Other Recent Discoveries About Human Sexuality" in the 1980s. It referred to an article from 1950 in the International Journal of Sexology in which gynecologist, Dr. Ernest Grafenberg wrote about erotic sensitivity along the anterior vaginal wall.

While many people have read or heard about Grafenberg, few have read his actual words. In reality, Grafenberg only uses the word "spot" twice and he uses it to make the opposite point to the way it has been popularly used. He states that "there is no spot in the female body, from which sexual desire could not be aroused. Innumerable erotogenic spots are distributed all over the body, from where sexual satisfaction can be elicited; these are so many that we can almost say that there is no part of the female body which does not give sexual response, the partner has only to find the erotogenic zones."

The Grafenberg spot (G-Spot) is said to be a sensitive area just behind the front wall of the vagina, between the back of the pubic bone and the cervix. Beverly Whipple, a certified sex educator and counselor, and John D. Perry, an ordained minister, psychologist, and sexologist, named the G-Spot after gynecologist Ernest Grafenberg (1881-1957).

Dr. Grafenberg was the first modern physician to describe the area and argue for its importance in female sexual pleasure. His claim is that when this spot is stimulated during sex through vaginal penetration of some kind (fingers during masturbation, penis or other object partly thrusting into the vagina), some women have an orgasm. This orgasm may include a gush of fluid from the urethra -- sometimes called the "female ejaculation" -- however, many experts do not agree on this. It is not considered urine. Is this real? Many gynecologists and physiologist still argue.

There has been a large amount of controversy among sex researchers regarding this theory. For women who have felt this gush of urethral fluid, or for those who have found a new pleasure spot, having a name for it confirms their experience.

But remember, not all women are sensitive in this area, so be careful not to set up unrealistic expectations for yourself. Try it out; if it works, great, if it doesn't seem sensitive, try to find the spot(s) that are right for you!

Multiple orgasms

It's no secret that many women have multiple orgasms. Masters and Johnson documented this occurrence more than 25 years ago. Every woman has the ability to achieve multiple orgasms!

Anyone who has one orgasm has the potential to have another- it's not some fluke of nature that just a select few

240

experience. Multiple orgasms may be more difficult to achieve, but that's when the partner's role comes into play…

A woman's ability to be multi-orgasmic depends on many factors that you can help her with:
• Her comfort level (with partner and with surroundings)
• Her energy-level (level of stress and fatigue)
• The sexual technique or position being used

Create a comfortable atmosphere, make sure she's stress-free, and ask her which position helps her achieve orgasm best. Talk about it.

Now, in order to help her become multi-orgasmic, it is important to be aware of the two types of multiple orgasms that she can experience…

1. Sequential Multiples
• A series of climaxes that come close together (2-10 minutes apart)
• There is an interruption in arousal before the first and second orgasm
• Common scenario for this type is oral sex climax followed by climax in intercourse

2. Serial Multiples
• Orgasms come one after the other (separated by seconds without interruption in arousal)
• Occurs during intercourse when all the right spots are being stimulated (like the clitoris and or, G-Spot).

Women who do experience multiple orgasms have a few things in common. They tend to be women who have examined their own genitalia and are familiar with their equipment. They tend to be women who masturbate frequently and engage in frequent sexual fantasies. They are more likely to have open and frank sexual discussions with their partners. Whether or not you want to experience multiple orgasms, you should emulate these multiply-orgasmic women. They have happy and fulfilling sexual lives, and that's a goal every woman should strive for.

The main point here is to continue to relax, take a deep breath after the first orgasm, and keep going. Work through the period of increased sensitivity. Ride it out. Stay focused on the pleasure. Partners should not change the tempo of the stimulation. Some experimentation and practice may be required.

Female Ejaculation

Females ejaculate? Yes, they do. The amount of fluid that flows out can go from a few drops to a few tablespoonfuls. Actually, to be more accurate, the fluid comes squirting out of her urethra. It's not urine. Female ejaculate is a clear, odorless liquid produced by a small organ called the "female prostate," or urethral sponge, which is located between the urethra and vagina.

While some women may experience ejaculation naturally in the course of intercourse or other sex play, most require some concentrated stimulation of the G-spot. Massaging the G-spot causes the urethral sponge to become engorged with fluid, which is then expelled during orgasm. And, as with an orgasm, ejaculation also requires the woman to "let go." Before ejaculating, the woman will feel as though she is going to urinate. However, it is nearly impossible for her to urinate while coming, because the muscular contractions of orgasm close off the bladder and prevent the passage of urine.

The most reliable way to induce female ejaculation is by manual stimulation. Lay a towel on the bed before you begin (the amount of fluid released can be considerable). Make sure your hands are clean and your nails well trimmed. Get into a comfortable position between her legs, as achieving ejaculation can take half an hour or more. Use lube if necessary to get started or in case she starts to feel dry. Begin by stroking or orally stimulating her clitoris to

242

get her aroused. Once she begins to get aroused, insert two fingers, palm side up, into her vagina. About an inch to two inches inside the vaginal entrance, you should feel a round, roughened area on the front wall. This is the G-spot. Stroke against this area using firm pressure. You should vary the pressure to suit her particular degree of sensitivity. It should enlarge and begin to feel more solid. Try touching or licking her clitoris as you manipulate the G-spot. Follow her responses and pace yourself to prolong her period of arousal.

As she gets closer to climaxing, she will start to feel as though she has to urinate. That's the ejaculate beginning to flow into her urethra. In order for her ejaculate, she has to relax, let go, and push down and out with the same muscles she would use as if she were urinating. It may be hard to overcome the impulse to hold back, but you can reassure her, again, that if she is climaxing, she will not urinate. Instead, as she comes and pushes the fluid out, she should feel extra intense orgasmic pleasure, and you should be rewarded with a spurt of nectar that may range from gentle gush to a drenching spray. The ejaculate is a complex carbohydrate necessary for the health of the vagina. Attaining female ejaculation may take some practice and experimentation.

While manual stimulation is the most reliable method, caressing her G-Spot with the head of the penis can also prove very effective. You may find it easier to stimulate her G-spot if she gets on her hands and knees and you enter her from behind, pressing down on the G-spot instead of up. As a woman gets more familiar with ejaculation and the sensations associated with it, it should be easier for her to achieve.

Not all women will have the capability of ejaculating or certainly not every time they have intercourse. It's not something that takes place every time a female experiences an orgasm either, so it does not reflect the quality or enjoyment of the sexual experience.

Male Orgasm

The subjective feeling of orgasm in men has been described quite consistently as beginning with the sensation of deep warmth or pressure that corresponds to ejaculatory inevitability, the point when ejaculation cannot be stopped. It is then felt as sharp, intensely pleasurable contractions involving the pc muscles, anal sphincter, rectum, perineum and genitals. Some men describe this part as a sensation of pumping. Finally, a warm rush of fluid or a shooting sensation describes the actual process of semen travelling through the urethra during ejaculation.

It is important to note that orgasm and ejaculation are not one in the same event. Although they typically occur together, a man may have an orgasm without ejaculating. Orgasm refers specifically to the sudden and rhythmic muscular contractions in the pelvic region that release accumulated sexual tension and result in an intensely pleasurable sensation.

Ejaculation is the release of semen from the penis. It is a normal part of the male sexual response cycle. During sexual intercourse or masturbation, semen collects in the ejaculatory ducts, which are located where the ends of the vas deferentia join the seminal vesicles within the prostate gland.

When excitation reaches its peak, a spinal reflex causes the rhythmic contractions of the smooth muscles within the urethra, penis and the prostate gland, and propels the semen through the urethra out the tip of the penis in spurts.

Once a man reaches a certain point of sexual arousal, he can no longer prevent ejaculation. This feeling of having reached the brink of control once these contractions start is known as ejaculatory inevitability.

The rhythmic contractions of the prostate, perineal muscles and shaft of the penis occur initially at 0.8-second intervals, just as in women, and account for the spurting action of the semen during ejaculation. The intervals between contractions become longer and the intensity of the contractions tapers off after the first three or four contractions.

The semen does not actually appear until a few seconds after the point of ejaculatory inevitability because of the distance the seminal fluid has to travel through the urethra. During ejaculation, the internal sphincter of the urinary bladder is tightly sealed to make sure that the seminal fluid travels forward and to prevent any urine from mixing with the semen.

Sometimes ejaculation occurs involuntarily and unbeknownst to the man during sleep. This is known as nocturnal emission or, in slang terms as a "wet dream" and is particularly common in adolescents and young men.

Types of Orgasms

In addition to the usual orgasm described in some detail above, men can also have the much more intense P-Spot orgasm. The tissue that forms the urethral sponge, or G-spot, in female anatomy forms the prostate, which you can think of as the male G-spot (or the "P-spot") in male anatomy. The prostate gland makes prostatic fluid and pumps it into the mix of fluids that flows out through the urethra, most often in tandem with orgasm.

The most direct route to prostate stimulation is through anal penetration. Just as rhythmic pressure on the front wall of the vagina gets at the G-spot, pressure on the front wall of the rectum gets at the P-spot. Anal play carries an undeserved stigma, but the potential for mind-blowing orgasms is more than worth the work of overcoming your anal reservations. Men who incorporate prostate stimulation into their sex lives report some of the same ecstatic sexual experiences as women who climax with G-spot stimulation.

Multiple Orgasms

Men can enjoy multiple orgasms if they stop or change the stimulation they are creating/receiving just prior to reaching the point of ejaculatory inevitability. If done close enough to ejaculation, he may experience the muscular contractions that constitute orgasm (including the 3-5 sec. "fluttering" muscular contractions in the pelvis) without moving into ejaculation and erection loss. Since he has avoided ejaculation, he will not enter the refractory period during which he is incapable of experiencing further orgasms.

First, strengthen the PC muscle using kegel exercises. The stronger the PC muscle, the more well-equipped to delay ejaculation. Take slow, deep breaths. At the same time, flex the PC muscle. Bring yourself to orgasm, but without ejaculating. There are several methods you can use to keep yourself from ejaculating, so try them all and see which work best:

- Squeeze the tip of the penis by making a ring around the glans (head)
- Squeeze the base of your penis
- Use your thumb and forefinger to circle your testicles and gently pull them away from your body
- Apply pressure against your perineum, the soft tissue between your testicles and your anus

The combination of deep breathing, relaxation, contraction of the pc muscle, and orgasm without ejaculation create an experience that many men describe as a "full-body orgasm." Men who use these techniques can eventually have multiple orgasms. Practicing these techniques will heighten your sexual sensations as well as your orgasms, whether or not you achieve multiple orgasms.

Types of Ejaculation

There are several types of ejaculation. In some cases, the fine-tuned process of this sexual response is disrupted.

Retrograde Ejaculation.

In a condition called retrograde ejaculation, the bladder's sphincter does not close off properly during ejaculation, so semen spurts backward into the bladder. This condition is usually found in some men who have multiple sclerosis, diabetes, or after some types of prostate surgery. It can also occasionally occur in men who do not have any serious problems. It is not physically harmful, but it does render the man infertile and he may have a different sensation during ejaculation. A retrograde ejaculation is also known as a "dry come" because the man may experience orgasm, but no semen is released from the penis.

Premature Ejaculation.

This condition, also known as rapid ejaculation, is a sexual response problem in which a man consistently feels he has little or no control over the timing of his buildup to ejaculation.

Retarded Ejaculation.

Also known as delayed ejaculation, this condition is a sexual response problem also known as ejaculatory incompetence in which a man is unable to ejaculate even though he is highly sexually aroused and wishes to ejaculate. This is not to be confused with the control needed for male multiple orgasms.

Dysfunction

Sexual dysfunction is difficulty during any stage of the sexual act that prevents the individual from enjoying sexual activity. Dysfunction is not to be confused with deviations.

Sexual difficulties can begin early in a person's sex life or they may develop after an individual has previously experienced enjoyable and satisfying sex. A problem may develop gradually over time, or may occur suddenly as a total or partial inability to participate in one or more stages of the sexual act. The causes of sexual difficulties can be physical, psychological, or both.

Emotional factors affecting sex include both interpersonal problems between partners and psychological problems within the individual. Being able to openly communicate with your partner can help resolve most problems in this area.

Physical factors include drugs, injuries to the back, problems with an enlarged prostate gland, problems with blood supply, nerve damage, or disease, failure of various organ systems, endocrine disorders, hormonal deficiencies, and some birth defects.

Sexual dysfunction disorders are generally classified into four categories: sexual desire disorders, sexual arousal disorders, orgasm disorders, and sexual pain disorders.

Sexual desire disorders or decreased libido can be caused by a decrease in normal estrogen (in women) or testosterone (in both men and women) production. Other causes may be aging, fatigue, pregnancy, medications or psychiatric conditions, such as depression and anxiety.

Sexual arousal disorders were previously known as frigidity in women and impotence in men, though these have now been replaced with less judgmental terms. Impotence is now known as erectile dysfunction, and frigidity has been replaced with a number of terms describing specific problems with, for example, desire or arousal. For both men and women, these conditions can manifest as an aversion to, and avoidance of, sexual contact with a partner. In men, there may be partial or complete failure to attain or maintain an erection, or a lack of sexual excitement and pleasure in sexual activity.

There may be medical causes to these disorders, such as decreased blood flow or lack of vaginal lubrication. Chronic disease can also contribute, as well as the nature of the relationship between the partners. As the success of sildenafil (Viagra) attests, most erectile disorders in men are primarily physical, not psychological conditions.

Orgasm disorders are a persistent delay or absence of orgasm following a normal sexual excitement phase. The disorder can occur in both women and men. The SSRI antidepressants are frequent culprits -- these can delay the achievement of orgasm or eliminate it entirely.

Sexual pain disorders affect women almost exclusively and are known as dyspareunia (painful intercourse) and vaginismus (an involuntary spasm of the muscles of the vaginal wall that interferes with intercourse). Dyspareunia may be caused by insufficient lubrication (vaginal dryness) in women. Poor lubrication may result from insufficient excitement and stimulation, or from hormonal changes caused by menopause, pregnancy, or breast-feeding. Irritation from contraceptive creams and foams can also cause dryness, as can fear and anxiety about sex.

Sexual dysfunctions are more common in the early adult years, with the majority of people seeking care for such conditions during their late twenties through thirties. The incidence increases again in the geriatric population, typically with gradual onset of symptoms that are associated most commonly with the medical and physical causes of sexual dysfunction.

Sexual dysfunction is more common in people who abuse alcohol and drugs. It is also more likely in people suffering from diabetes and degenerative neurological disorders. Ongoing psychological problems, difficulty maintaining relationships or chronic disharmony with the current sexual partner can also interfere with sexual function.

Since people tend not to talk to one another about their sexual problems, many people imagine that they are "abnormal", or that their sexual problems are unique or shameful. Images of sexuality presented by society and the media often present people with unrealistic ideals of sexual behavior, whether of the ideals of chastity and sexual fidelity presented by religion, or the ideal of sexual inexhaustibility and promiscuous availability presented by pornography. Neither image appears to be representative of human behavior in real life: this has been summed up in the phrase *"everyone lies about sex"*. Speaking frankly with your physician, and your partner, is the best way to solve sexual problems.

References

Society for Human Sexuality

http://www.gspotcenter.com/facts/prostate-spot

http://www.sex-ed101.org

Addiego, F., Belzer, E. G., Comolli, J., Moger, W., Perry, J. D., & Whipple, B. (1981). Female ejaculation: A case study. *The Journal of Sex Research*, 17, 13-21.

Arthur, Clint (2004) "9 Free Secrets of New Sensual Power"

Nicola Jones (2002-07-03). "Bigger is better when it comes to the G spot". *New Scientist*. Retrieved on 2006-06-29.

Female Ejaculation. Retrieved on 2006-08-26.

Sundahl, D. (February 2003). *Female Ejaculation and the G-Spot*. Hunter House Publishers. ISBN 0-89793-380-X.

Regnier De Graaf, New Treatise Concerning the Generative Organs of Women

Edwin G. Belzer, Jr., Beverly Whipple and William Moger, co-researchers with Addiego, et al (1981)

Gary Schubach, Ed.D 2001, Urethral Expulsions During Sensual Arousal and Bladder Catheterization in Seven Human Females

Cabello, F. (1997). Female ejaculation: Myth and reality. In J.J. Baras-Vass & M.Perez-Conchillo (Eds) Sexuality and Human Rights: Proceedings of the XIII World Congress of Sexology (pp.325-333) Valencia, Spain: E.C.V.S.A.

Female Ejaculation. Citing The Lovers' Guide (2006-08-26). Retrieved on 2006-08-26.

CEG (2001) National guidelines on the management of Trichomoniasis vaginalis. Clinical Effectiveness Group

(Association of Genitourinary Medicine and the Medical Society for the Study of Venereal Diseases)

Female Ejaculation: Research Contrary to BBFC Ruling

SexTutor.com

Sinclair Intimacy Institute

http://www.femaleorgasm.md

Masters, W.H.; Johnson, V.E. (1966). *Human Sexual Response*. Toronto; New York: Bantam Books. ISBN 0-553-20429-7.

Masters, W.H.; Johnson, V.E. (1970). *Human Sexual Inadequacy*. Toronto; New York: Bantam Books. ISBN 0-553-20699-0.

Masters, W.H.; Johnson, V.E. (1974). *The Pleasure Bond*. Toronto; New York: Bantam Books. ISBN 0-553-20915-9.

Masters, W.H.; Johnson, V.E. (1979). *Homosexuality in Perspective*. Toronto; New York: Bantam Books. ISBN 0-553-20809-8.

Wikipedia

Exton, MS; et al. (April 2001). "Coitus-induced orgasm stimulates prolactin secretion in healthy subjects". Psychoneuroendocrinology 26 (3): 287 – 94. Retrieved on 2006-05-28.

Sobrinho, LG (2003). "Prolactin, psychological stress and environment in humans: adaptation and maladaptation". *Pituitary* **6** (1): 35 – 9. Retrieved on 2006-05-28.

Georgiadis J, Kortekaas R, Kuipers R, Nieuwenburg A, Pruim J, Reinders A, Holstege G (2006). "Regional cerebral blood flow changes associated with clitorally induced orgasm in healthy women". *Eur J Neurosci* 24(11): 3305-16. PMID 17156391.

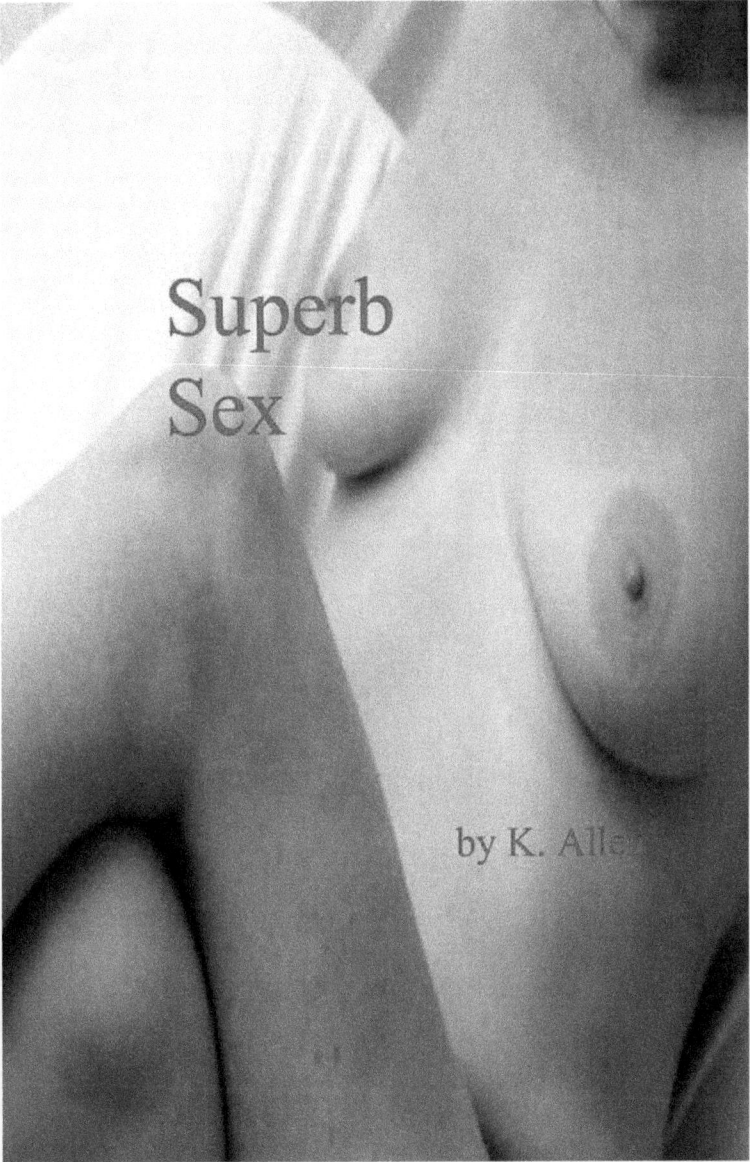

Superb
Sex

by K. Alle

by Camden C. Cochran

for everyone

Introduction

You may think you know everything I am about to tell you and you may be right but there are many who do not know and only think they do. I have experienced more than most when it comes to sexual congress. I tell you that most people have no idea how overwhelmingly good sex, just straight old regular sex, can actually be.

There are several reasons for this. Lack of experience, lack of sensitivity, a limited number of skilled and/or attentive partners, unlimited egotism, even the attitude that sex is bad or nasty – they all contribute to sexual incompetence. I have even heard some women say that sex is for younger people only and that they have moved beyond needing sex.

That last reason for not having sex is patently false. Physical intimacy is a necessary ingredient in all intimate relationships even those between elderly persons. A woman I know who is in her late 40's stated, without reservation, that the best lover she has ever had was a man in his 70's. Age, fitness levels, medical issues, and handicaps are no reasons to stop enjoying sex. You may have to modify your technique and be inventive but that should not be a deterrent.

One does not have to be "in love" in order to enjoy superb sex. There should be some level of attraction, affection, and some comfort between the partners but a deep emotional attachment is not necessary. This is not a book on relationships. This is a book dealing just with how to have superb sex.

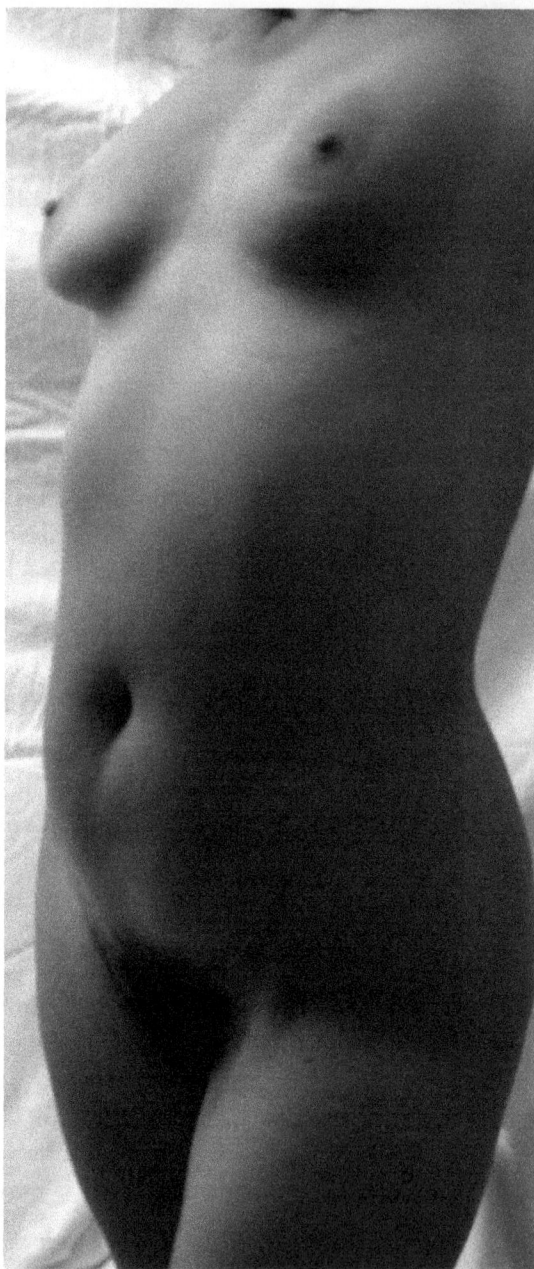

by C. Cochran

Preparation

1. Safe sex
2. Birth control
3. Venue
4. Attitude

One has to be prepared to have sex. One has to desire sex and have a partner who desires sex and is also prepared. This means that you and your partner both know your health status. Are you both free from disease and illness?
Even a cold will have a negative impact upon your enjoyment. Do you have birth control and condoms available? Both are required for heterosexual activity. Condoms are not used to prevent pregnancy, although they will; condoms are used to prevent the possible transmission of disease since some diseases have long incubation periods and your partner may not be exhibiting any symptoms. Better safe than dead. Men should know what size of condoms they require. Some people are allergic to latex. If you are one of these people, polyurethane condoms are available. There are websites that will make custom condoms if you require them both in latex and polyurethane. Condoms do work very well when properly used. Not using condoms is not an option unless you are trying to make her pregnant.

Birth control pills do not cause breast cancer. Birth control pills make your body think you are pregnant. The risks associated with taking birth control pills are the same risks as those associated with being pregnant. There are a variety of pills available. See your doctor. There are other effective birth control methods available if taking birth control pills is not an option for you. Once again, see your doctor. Not using an effective birth control method is not an option unless you are trying to become pregnant.

If either prospective partner is in any way unprepared for sex you should not have sex. Saying "No, thank you" is always an option for either partner.

Next comes the venue. A strong bed with a firm mattress and clean sheets is the preferred location but there are other venues. Privacy is always a wise choice. Easy access to a bathroom is another good idea although it is not mandatory. Sex is often a messy business however and it requires some clean-up. Bear this in mind when selecting a venue.

Attitude is the final element. Each person simply must be willing to enjoy sex to its fullest. If you think sex is dirty, gross, nasty, bad, or even evil, you will not enjoy sex. If the relationship between the partners is fraught with distrust or discord, the sex will be poor quality. If either partner is unwilling to express their desire to its fullest, the sex will not be as good as it could, and should, be. If you have any inhibitions when it comes to sex, the time to discuss and deal with them is before you start. Fear, of any kind or for any reason, will ruin the experience. If you or your partner have any reservations, discuss them beforehand or call the whole thing off.

Never be afraid to have sex but never be afraid to not have sex. One does not have to settle for any sex just to have sex. If you find yourself having problems, consult a medical professional, a marriage counselor, or a sex therapist.

Men

Men are not machines. They are people therefore they are not going to be perfect. That being said, a certain amount of sexual skill should be expected from them.

1. Massage/erotic massage
2. Body worship
3. Cunnilingus
4. Manual stimulation of clitoris and G-Spot
5. Stimulation of the G-Spot and posterior fornix with his penis

Those are the basics for heterosexual activity. Each woman differs in the details of what she enjoys but the general physiognomy is the same. Some exploration of each woman will be required. This will take time and perhaps a bit of coaching from the woman involved. Ladies please remember that men like to please their partners and they do like receiving any help you could give them.

Foreplay is mandatory. Foreplay begins with the mind of your partner. Catch and ignite her/his interest. Kissing, nuzzling, and cuddling moves into disrobing and then massage or erotic massage which gives way to body worship and so on. Everything up to actual penetration /intercourse can be considered foreplay. Even putting on the condom can become part of foreplay. Both men and women should know how to handle condoms. Do not stint on the foreplay since orgasms for women are strongly linked to the degree of her arousal. The more aroused she is, the easier it is for her to orgasm. One orgasm tends to lead to another and then another. Each woman should expect to receive at least three orgasms per sexual experience although having an orgasm is not entirely necessary for her to enjoy the experience.

Once you have gotten her thoroughly aroused using body worship move to manual stimulation of her clitoris, then cunnilingus, then cunnilingus with manual stimulation of her G-Spot. She should have one orgasm during cunnilingus alone and another during cunnilingus with G-Spot stimulation. She may or may not ejaculate. Female ejaculation is never guaranteed but it usually occurs during G-Spot stimulation and/or when using the female superior position during intercourse.

Now is the time for the condom. Lubricate only the head of your penis and roll the condom on completely leaving the tip ready to receive your semen. Then lubricate the outside of the condom lightly. She may be willing to help with this operation and should be encouraged to do so.

Using just the head of your penis begin gently caressing her G-Spot pressing upwards. The speed and the pressure will vary between women. If she did not yet have a second orgasm, now would be an excellent time to help her achieve this one. Do not move to her posterior fornix until she has had two, or more, orgasms.

Should she become hyper-sensitive after having an orgasm, do not stop. Just lighten up and slow down a bit. What she thinks as pain is a false signal. The higher levels of stimulation are being incorrectly interpreted by her brain. Encourage her to breathe deeply and calmly and to relax. Ride the period of hyper-sensitivity out. In severe cases, return to body worship until she has calmed down and relaxed.

After the G-Spot orgasm, find her cervix and slide under it. Some women enjoy being banged on their cervix but you're hitting bone which most do not like. It hurts. Never ride up and over her cervix. Going above can lead to serious injury leading to the emergency room and an operating theatre. Stay down and slide on in to the back.

This is the location of her posterior fornix. Gently begin caressing this area pressing downward. Once again, the speed and pressure desired will vary between women. She should have her third, if not more, orgasm now. Men with excellent control can then alternate between her G-Spot and her posterior fornix helping her to achieve more orgasms.

These areas are the same regardless of the position used. Some positions more closely target one area over another but most can be reached in any position if you are clever enough. A wise man learns to tell where he is in relation to her when he is inside of her. A wise also learns how to 'listen' to a woman's body and to read her unspoken physical signals. These skills are learned through practice.

When it is time for him to orgasm, many men find they have a second gear when thrusting toward their climax. This can also induce orgasms in their partner. At this point, encourage him on to orgasm. If some additional stimulation is required, supply it. Sex is supposed to be a mutually enjoyable experience.

However, men are not machines. Upon occasion, his erection will fail or he will be unable to achieve orgasm. In either case, this is no one's fault. Kindness, understanding, and consideration are needed. A man can still thrill his partner using other methods and while an orgasm is highly desirable, it is not necessary for his overall enjoyment of the experience.

Each partner is responsible for their own orgasms. Your partner is supposed to help but is not responsible for their achievement. This is where attitude comes in. A pro-sex attitude is required. A willingness to orgasm, to enjoy sex is required. No one can 'give' or 'make' another person orgasm.

Women

Most cultures of the world teach women to curb and deny their sexuality. Therefore, a woman's attitude toward sex directly impacts her enjoyment. Good women do enjoy sex. Give yourself permission to enjoy sex. The clitoris, the G-Spot and the posterior fornix have no other function except the enjoyment of sex. They are not necessary for your health. They are not necessary for having children. They only exist to give you sexual delight when properly stimulated.

Every woman should have basic sexual skills which include

1. Massage/erotic massage
2. Body Worship
3. Fellatio
4. The Female Superior position
5. Prostate (P-Spot) massage

You will notice that items 1 and 2 are the same for every - one. Reciprocity is necessary for superb sex. Men enjoy being caressed and worshipped just as much as women do so do not be shy about touching and caressing him. Men should encourage women to participate fully in the sexual experience as an active, even an aggressive, partner. Encourage men to guide you as each man will be different in what he enjoys.

Being slow to arouse and being slow to orgasm is nothing a woman should take pride in being. You are only denying yourself pleasure and decreasing his. Men want just as enthusiastic and skilled a lover as you do. Being multi-orgasmic and not afraid to ejaculate is what you want to become. Good women do enjoy sex and they are good at sex.

Fellatio is easier if the woman controls the motion. Whether to swallow semen or not is a personal choice. Most men would prefer that you do but it remains your choice if you do fellatio with the aim of inducing his climax. If you are doing it as part of foreplay you will want to stop and move on before he climaxes.

The motion used when in the female superior position is up and forward then down and back using your knees as the fulcrum. Some practice is necessary. If you are using a bed, you can use the bounce to help create and then to sustain the motion. He can also assist by moving his hips upward with you. There is also a 'scrubbing' motion of the hips that rubs your clitoris against him. Men are highly visually oriented and may enjoy watching you caress yourself should you desire to do so. This is also your choice. Men also tend to enjoy the movements of your breasts when using this position. There is no need to hold back your sexual response at any time if you both enjoy it.

Prostate massage is a delicate subject because to access the anterior portion of the prostate gland, which is where his P-Spot is located, requires insertion into his rectum. A vibrating anal probe is the best tool to use for this but fingers will do. Using lubricant is recommended. Be careful if you have long fingernails. Do not scratch him here. Washing up immediately afterward is required any time the rectum is used during sex including after anal sex with him inside of her. Gently slide upward and caress while pressing toward his stomach. Speed and pressure will vary between men. Some men will be hesitant to allow P-Spot massage. Their wishes must be accepted. It is his choice.

Men have a refractory period after ejaculation. This is when he has to rest and recover. Many men also become hyper-sensitive and cannot bear to have their penis touched at this time. Just as with women, this is a false signal. However, he really is incapable of another erection at this time so refraining from touching him is best. It is possible for a man to become multi-orgasmic but in order to do this, he has to orgasm without ejaculating.

Now is the time to rest, clean-up, and cuddle. If desired, after he has recovered, you both can do it all again. Most women experience an upsurge in their energy level after sex but this is not the case with men. Finding a balance that satisfies you both may take some time but taking this time is well worth the effort. As you both become more familiar with eachother you find it easier to have superb sex with eachother. Periods of hyper-sensitivity and incidence of erection failure diminish and will, in most cases, entirely disappear as the level of trust, acceptance, and comfort grows between the partners.

There is the idea that becoming familiar leads to the sex becoming boring. This only happens if you are not paying attention. Even with the same partner, sex is subtly different each and every time. Some days are better than others, of course, since neither person is a machine but there is a charm to sex with a reliable partner who knows your combination and style. Everyone grows and changes over time. Your partner may not be the same person he or she was earlier. It is impossible to completely know another person. As they mature further, there is more to know. Continued exploration and continued communication are the keys to keeping sex superb over the long term.

Body Worship

There are two reasons to use body worship the first being to make him yours. Once a man has experienced body worship as done by a skilled soft domme, nothing else ever comes close. The second reason is have him body worship you to increase his obedience and to train him to "listen" to a woman's body.

You begin with him lying face down with a pillow slightly elevating his upper chest for comfort. The idea is to both relax and arouse him while discovering exactly what works with his body. Start at his head and slowly kiss, nibble, lick, suck, bite, caress with trailing tresses, lips, tongue, hands, claws, and your body all the way down his. Slowly means agonizingly slowly. Vary the sides, the direction of movement, the pressure as you trace graceful arabesques along his skin. Make a careful mental note of what he and his body likes and dislikes in the way of touch. He is not permitted to move during body worship. He must learn to accept your caress. If you leave slight claw marks make a note later of how fast they disappear.

Have a look at a man's anatomy. The nerves form a network that you can follow. Tracing up his spine with a slightly moist tongue tip and ending with a passionately wet and heavy kiss onto the nape of his neck while holding his shoulders tightly in your arms is most effective both from a nerve stimulating point of view but also from a psychological view, this movement being how a cat kills its prey – the bite to the back of the neck. A man is vulnerable in this position. Such small motions can have profound effects.

Also note how his muscles run and how each connects to the bone. The heaviest pressures should only be applied to areas of heavy muscle or directly onto bone. A man' shoulders and thighs are usually heavily muscled. Beware of applying any pressure onto his joints. When pressing onto bone move along the bone; for example, the femur, the large thigh bone, runs up and down and bears the weight of his body along its length. Pressure across the bone might cause damage while pressure along the bone will not. When 'Stroking the Bones', always move along the bone in the direction of their strength.

Another movement is slowly licking up the backs of his legs from the ankles to his rump. If you lave moisture behind, gently blow onto his skin. This will dry the moisture and chill that bit of skin adding more stimuli. If he has scars, they will usually be sensitive. You can use this sensitivity to great effect as well. Tickling is not desirable. Remember while you are doing this to take the time to appreciate the planes and angles of his body, the feel of his skin, the hardness of his muscles – whatever delights you since you may want to compliment him or remark on it later. Murmurs of appreciation and encouragement during body worship are optional.

Now it is time for him to roll over. Once again begin at the head; kissing the outer corners of his eyes, nibbling his neck, kissing his throat, tracing the outline of his lips with a dry tongue-tip, etc. Gradually work your way down, do not neglect his fingers and toes either, but do NOT touch his genitals. Take your time and note nuances – learn to "listen" to his body.

Explore him. Experiment upon him. Enjoy him.

Both genders enjoy body worship and it is the single most effective way to simultaneously relax and arouse your partner. Including body worship with intercourse itself, for example when her legs are over or on your shoulder lick her ankles or kiss her instep, makes the entire experience more erotic and sensual.

Small Items

Here are a few subtle ways to signal to your desire, and your skill level, to your partner when out in public. Every long term partnership develops their own set of signals, naturally, but for those who have yet to establish theirs here are a few things you can do.

Eye Kiss
Instead of going for the lips, gently and slowly kiss with just a hint of tongue tip the outer corner of his or her eye. You can make it appear as if you were whispering to him or her. Make sure to hold the kiss for 10 seconds.

Finger Caress
While holding hands is nice, interlacing your fingers and slowly and gently sliding yours between his/hers is provocative and sensual.

Promising
Rest your fingertips on the back of his/her hand gently and hold eye contact for approximately 20 seconds. Then let go. And alternative 'promise' is to stand next to him/her and to lightly place the palm of your hand on his/her back just above the small of his/her back. Do not hug; just rest it there while you make and hold eye contact for 20 seconds. Once again, let go.

These small items will work regardless of the genders involved. They signal sexual interest with grace and a hint of sensuality that is sure to capture and focus your partner's interest.

Sexual Fitness

You do not have to be in peak physical condition to enjoy superb sex. It helps, but it is not mandatory. There is always something you and your partner can do. Become inventive and imaginative.

One thing you do have to be is properly hydrated especially if you are male. Men depend upon hydraulics and their hydraulics will fail if he is dehydrated. Water remains the best choice for hydration.

Leg cramps and/or muscle weakness indicate a lack of potassium in your diet. Vitamins will help here.

Being rested beforehand also helps since superb sex is usually rather active and prolonged. There is nothing "quickie" about this. You have to focus your mind outward toward your partner and you cannot do this if you are exhausted.

Other than that, whatever shape you're in will be just fine.

The Program

Your guide to wild rampant skin-on-skin full-body-contact sex.

1. massage
2. erotic massage/necking
3. body worship
4. manual stimulation
5. cunnilingus/fellatio
6. cunnilingus/fellatio with manual stimulation of the G-Spot/P-Spot
7. G-Spot caressing using the penis
8. posterior fornix caressing using the penis
9. alternate between the G-Spot and the posterior fornix for as long as he can hold out

if a break between her orgasms is needed return to body worship to keep her warm

10. time for his climax
11. cuddle
12. rest

Repeat three times per session.
Have three sessions per week.

Spending time on 1,2, and 3 guarantees completion on 4 through 10.
Proper outercourse leads to intercourse.
Take turns "leading" with your partner.

Sexual Exercises

Exercises in Spatial Awareness
1. Vertical Massage: with her standing before you, begin at the ankles and work your way up, using body oils warmed by being rubbed between your palms while blindfolded.
2. Erotic Massage: as above except she's lying down and no oil is used.
3. G-Spot Stimulation: kneeling between her spread thighs, slowly enter her and caress her G-Spot with the head of your penis while blindfolded until she orgasms twice.
4. Posterior Fornix: as above except now aim for the posterior fornix and caress there until she orgasms twice.

Given his generally larger size and heavier weight, a gentleman must know where he is in relation to the lady at all times both inside of her and outside of her to prevent discomfort and accidents. Ladies wishing to reciprocate, delight, and explore their gentlemen, should practice exercise 2 as above. To sensitize him, the lady should blindfold him, not herself, before doing exercise 2.

Exercises in Acceptance
1. Tactile Denial: cuff his hands behind him before enjoying sex with him.
2. Denying Movement: in the female superior position, stop if he moves. If he finds this too difficult, have him sit with his back up against the headboard and tie his hands to either side before riding him.

Here the goal is for both partners to understand and accept that the leading role is not strictly a masculine prerogative. In this way, both begin to see a lady as an equal and active partner. His acceptance of her sexuality also increases her trust in him. Please note that restraints should only be used in exercise 2 if needed or desired.

Exercises in Multi-tasking
1. Hot Spots: he must use his mouth, one hand, and his penis all at once to simultaneously caress three widely separated hot spots.
2. Total Stimulation: when coming in from behind, his must use both of his hands, his mouth, his voice, and his penis to caress, stimulate, tantalize, and hold the lady.

Some gentlemen are focused upon penetration, and this is simply not sufficiently skilled to meet the requirements of most ladies. Superb sex fully engages both partners' bodies and minds. These exercises will expand his focus. All of these exercises will help him learn how to 'listen' to a woman's body and increase his awareness of his own.

Conclusion

Sexual skills are not developed by anything other than practice. You simply must get out there with one exception. Women must masturbate to climax and learn themselves before engaging in sex with others. Women have to learn what an orgasm is, how it feels, and what she needs to achieve orgasm; first on her own and then with another.

After this, practice makes perfect and practicing has never been such fun!